corporate design international

Wolfgang Schmittel

Definition and benefit
of a consistent corporate
appearance

Definition und Nutzen
eines konsequenten
Firmenauftritts

Définition et valeur
d'une identité d'entreprise
intégrée et harmonieuse

ABC Edition Zurich

ABC Verlag Zürich

Editions ABC Zurich

© 1984 by ABC Edition, Zurich
ISBN 3-85504-080-X
Printed in Switzerland

© 1984 by ABC Verlag, Zürich
ISBN 3-85504-080-X
Gedruckt in der Schweiz

© 1984 by ABC Editions, Zurich
ISBN 3-85504-080-X
Imprimé en Suisse

Contents   Inhalt   Sommaire

There are two things upon which success under all circumstances rests. The one is that purpose and goal of the activity have been correctly defined, and the other is to find the correct actions towards that goal.

Es gibt zwei Dinge, auf denen das Wohlgelingen in allen Verhältnissen beruht.
Das eine ist, dass Zweck und Ziel der Tätigkeit richtig bestimmt sind, das andere aber besteht darin, die zu diesem Endziel führenden Handlungen zu finden.

Il y a deux choses sur lesquelles la réussite repose en toutes circonstances.
L'une réside dans la détermination judicieuse du but et du sens de l'action, l'autre consiste à découvrir les actes précis permettant d'atteindre l'objectif prévu.

Aristoteles

Thoughts of and a Vow for Corporate Identity, for Corporate Design

There are designed, intentional corporate appearances — and others that have come into existence rather by coincidence.
Already in the early fifties Braun, it is said, had such a corporate personality consistently planned for all areas — and so did e.g. Lufthansa and Olivetti. Certainly there were others, but not many and perhaps also not as consistently planned.
The term "CI" or Corporate Identity was not yet known at that time. This came up much later together with the Marketing language. Today almost everybody uses the term, which only touches upon advertising communication.

There are many definitions
One of them is contained in the CI book by Birkigt/Stadler:
"We see Corporate Identity in parallel to personal identity as a conclusive combination between appearance, words, actions of a company, and its character, or expressed more specifically, as a combination between corporate conduct, corporate appearance, corporate communication, and the hypostasized corporate personality as the manifested self-understanding of the company."
As the term is English I have consulted "Cassell's Dictionary" as a competent translator:
"Identity" = conformity, individuality
"Corporate" = unified, united, mutual effort, also guild, trade association. Or slang: paunch.
After citing all of these eloquent definitions I should like to add my own:

Gedanken und Bekenntnis zur Corporate Identity – zum Corporate Design

Es gibt gestaltete, beabsichtigte Firmenerscheinungsbilder –, und eher zufällig entstandene.
Braun, sagt man, hatte schon in den frühen fünfziger Jahren solch eine bewusst über alle Bereiche hinweg geplante «personality» – eine Firmenpersönlichkeit –, die Lufthansa zum Beispiel und Olivetti auch. Sicher noch einige, aber nicht viele und vielleicht auch nicht so konsequent.
Den Begriff «CI» oder «Corporate Identity» kannte man damals noch gar nicht. Der ist erst viel später mit der Sprache des Marketings aufgetaucht. Heute führt ihn fast jeder im Munde, der auch nur am Rande mit werblicher Kommunikation zu tun hat.

Es gibt viele Definitionen
Eine davon stammt aus dem CI-Buch von Birkigt/Stadler:
«Wir sehen die Corporate Identity in Parallele zur Ich-Identität als schlüssigen Zusammenhang von Erscheinung, Worten und Taten eines Unternehmens mit seinem Wesen, oder spezifischer ausgedrückt, von Unternehmensverhalten, Unternehmenserscheinungsbild und Unternehmenskommunikation mit der hypostasierten Unternehmenspersönlichkeit als dem manifestierten Selbstverständnis des Unternehmens.»
Da der Begriff aus dem Englischen stammt, habe ich «Cassell's Dictionary» als kompetenten Übersetzer genommen:
«Identity» = die Identität, die Gleichheit, Individualität,
«Corporate» = vereinigt, verbunden, vereinte Bemühung, auch Gilde, Zunft, Handelsgesellschaft.
Im Slang = der Schmerbauch.
Nach dieser Lektüre möchte ich zu all den eloquenten Auslegungen noch meine beisteuern.

Considérations générales et plaidoyer pour une Corporate Identity – un Corporate Design

Certaines images d'identification sont sciemment conçues pour une entreprise donnée, d'autres sont plutôt le fruit du hasard.
Dès le début des années cinquante, Braun possédait déjà – dit-on – une «personality», créée et planifiée dans le dessein d'englober tous les secteurs de l'entreprise. Il en était de même pour la Lufthansa, et aussi pour Olivetti, peut-être pour d'autres entreprises encore, pas très nombreuses.
L'expression «CI», ou «Corporate Identity», était encore inconnue à l'époque. Elle a fait son apparition beaucoup plus tard, avec le langage du marketing. De nos jours, elle est dans la bouche de tout le monde, même de ceux qui n'ont que rarement à faire à la communication publicitaire.

Les définitions sont nombreuses
L'une d'elles est extraite de l'ouvrage de Birkigt/Stadler, consacré à la CI:
«Par analogie à l'identité du Moi, nous voyons la Corporate Identity comme la corrélation concluante entre l'apparence, les paroles et actes d'une entreprise et sa nature inhérente ou, en termes plus spécifiques, entre le comportement, l'image d'identification et la communication de l'entreprise et sa personnalité hypostatique, qui exprime la manière dont l'entreprise se conçoit et se manifeste.»
Vu que l'expression vient de l'anglais, j'ai interrogé le dictionnaire sur la signification des termes:
«Identity» = identité, égalité, individualité
«Corporate» = corps constitué, corporation, personne ou personnalité morale, civile, juridique, raison sociale. Familier: bedaine, bedon.
Après toutes ces interprétations éloquentes, le lecteur me permettra d'ajouter quelques considérations de mon propre cru.

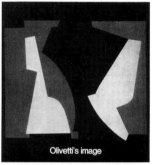

This is what makes Corporate Identity:
Equal intentions of all responsible parties. Cumulative effect. Intensive appearance. More credibility. More power of conviction. More successful work!

CI is a comprehensive, all-comprising ''formation''
It is corporate personality in the widest sense. Trade relationships, product, communal politics, personnel planning and administration, buildings, customer service, e. g. *the entire communication* from the TV spot over packaging and advertisement to the trade fair stand. This can also be read in the theoretical CI books.

To me, however, CI is primarily a matter of attitude, a matter of character!
A self-comprehension that comes from inside combined with a clear vision of the goal.
Designers can then transfer this mental attitude to a graphic picture — to ''CD'', i.e. ''Corporate Design''.
In this way purely aesthetic, qualitative aspects create economic values and success. The quality, which from own long-standing experience, I attribute to CI.

Missing self-comprehension leads to a mendacious picture of an artificial ''Corporate Design''.
Or, what is even worse: there will be no corporate appearance and every new advertising campaign will have *a new "advertising personality"*, and that is uneconomical! A true Corporate Identity does not form itself in an advertising agency. It requires a responsible center point.
Otherwise it will become an interchangeable advertising ''paunch''.

Das macht eine Corporate Identity aus:
Gleiche Absicht aller Verantwortlichen. Kumulative Wirkung. Intensives Auftreten. Mehr Glaubhaftigkeit. Grössere Überzeugungskraft. Erfolgreicheres Wirtschaften!

CI ist ein umfassendes, alles erfassendes «Gebilde»
Sie ist Unternehmenspersönlichkeit im weitesten Sinne. Handelsbeziehungen, Produkt, Kommunalpolitik, Personalwesen, Gebäude, Kundendienst zum Beispiel und *die gesamte Kommunikation,* vom TV-Spot über die Packung und Anzeige bis zum Messestand. Soweit ist das auch nachzulesen in den theoretischen CI-Werken.

Für mich ist CI aber vor allem eine Frage der Haltung, des Charakters!
Ein von innen heraus kommendes Selbstverständnis, verbunden mit einer klaren Zielvorstellung.
Designer können dies geistige Bild dann in ein grafisches übersetzen, ins Gestalterisch-Kommunikative, in ein «CD» – ein «Corporate Design».
So entstehen durch rein ästhetisch-qualitative Aspekte wiederum geschäftliche Werte und Erfolge. Die Güte, die ich einer CI aus eigener jahrelanger Erfahrung heraus zuschreibe.

Fehlendes Selbstverständnis führt zu einem verlogenen Bild oder aufgesetztem «Corporate Design».
Oder, was noch schlimmer ist: Es entsteht gar kein Firmen-Erscheinungsbild, sondern es gibt von Werbekampagne zu Werbekampagne *eine neue «Advertising Personality»*. Eine wahrhaftige Unternehmens-Identity bildet sich nicht in einer Werbeagentur. Dazu bedarf es einer verantwortlichen Zentrale. Sonst wird's ein austauschbarer Werbe-«Schmerbauch».

Traits saillants d'une Corporate Identity:
Intention commune de tous les responsables. Action cumulative. Présentation intensive. Crédibilité accrue. Effet persuasif renforcé. Chances de réussite multipliées!

CI est une entité qui englobe tout, qui intègre tout
Elle reflète la personnalité de l'entreprise, au sens large du terme, les relations commerciales, le produit, la politique communale, la politique du personnel, les bâtiments, le service après-vente et *l'ensemble de la communication,* depuis les spots télévisés, le conditionnement et l'annonce jusqu'au stand d'exposition.

Pour moi, la CI est cependant avant tout une question de comportement, de caractère!
C'est la perception de la nature profonde de l'entreprise, associée à des objectifs clairement définis.
Le designer, créateur en esthétique industrielle, sait traduire cette image de l'esprit en une forme communicative, un «CD» – ou «Corporate Design».
Des aspects purement esthétiques et qualitatifs engendrent à nouveau des valeurs et succès commerciaux, confirmant ainsi cette qualité spécifique que j'attribue à une CI.

La perception erronée de la véritable identité mène à une image mensongère ou à un «Corporate Design» incompatible avec la réalité.
Pire encore: il se développe *une nouvelle «advertising personality»* d'une campagne publicitaire à l'autre. L'identité véritable d'une entreprise requiert l'intervention d'une centrale responsable. Sinon, le résultat est un «bedon» publicitaire interchangeable.

Westinghouse Corporate Design Center

The Corporate Design Center's purpose is to help the Company achieve good, functional designs and a unified and contemporary appearance for all products, buildings, and graphic material.

Introduction

Originally, this book was meant to be titled "corporate identity international"; however, the longer I worked on this book, and the more documentation we gathered, weighed and compared, the more obvious became two aspects:

1. There is no such thing as an internationally maintained CI

● Hardly any company — not even those putting much importance on design — is in a position to consistently maintain one CI *internationally*. And definitely not with regard to print advertising.

● A large internationally known company (which we had contacted for a contribution) advised us that corporate appearances and product advertising were "handled" independently by the responsible persons in the countries, and that headquarters do not coordinate the individual markets. (Obviously the home country only delivers the name.) Participation in the book was therefore not possible.

● An internationally well-known CI agency replied that their design program does not hold good for advertising — but that advertising is a matter of advertising agencies and thus independent of their development of a corporate appearance! We have therefore left out this case study here, although their work was excellent otherwise.

● Merck's Design Directives, for instance, expressly state: "Design deviations from the basic line are possible and necessary in day-to-day product advertising."
Really? I don't think so at all. *Then we don't need design directives; then there is no CI,* and no Corporate Design.

Zur Einführung

Ursprünglich sollte dieses Buch «corporate identity international» heissen, aber je länger ich an dem Buch arbeitete und je mehr Material wir zusammentrugen, gegenüberstellten und verglichen, desto deutlicher wurden zwei Aspekte:

1. Es gibt keine international durchgehaltene CI

● Kaum eine Firma – selbst solche mit hohem Designanspruch – kann eine CI offenbar *international* konsequent verwirklichen. Schon gar nicht in der Anzeigenwerbung.

● Wir hörten von einem grossen, international bekannten Unternehmen (das wir wegen eines Beitrags anschrieben), dass Corporate-Auftritte und die Produktwerbung von den Länderverantwortlichen eigenständig «geführt» würden und das Stammhaus keine Koordination über einzelne Märkte vornähme. (Offenbar kommt nur noch der Name aus dem Mutterland.) Eine Beteiligung im Buch sei ihnen deshalb nicht möglich.

● Wir hörten von einer international renommierten CI-Agentur, dass ihr Design-Programm nicht für die Werbung gelte – sondern dass Reklame eine Sache der Werbeagenturen und somit unabhängig von der Entwicklung ihres Erscheinungsbildes sei! Also haben wir diese Fallstudie aus dem Buch gestrichen, obwohl die Arbeit sonst exzellent war!

● Im Heft der Gestaltungsrichtlinien von Merck ist zum Beispiel ausdrücklich vermerkt: «In der aktuellen Produktwerbung sind gestalterische Abweichungen von der Grundlinie möglich und nötig.»
Wirklich? Das finde ich ganz und gar nicht. *Dann braucht man keine Gestaltungsrichtlinien, dann ist es eben keine CI* und kein Corporate Design.

Introduction

A l'origine, le présent ouvrage devait porter le titre «corporate identity international». Mais au fur et à mesure que j'avançais dans la préparation de ce livre et que la documentation recueillie, comparée et triée s'accumulait, deux aspects ressortaient clairement:

1. Il n'existe pas de CI de caractère vraiment international

● Pratiquement aucune société – pas même celle qui a des ambitions graphiques élevées – ne peut appliquer systématiquement une CI *internationale*. Dans la publicité-presse, cette éventualité est totalement exclue.

● Une entreprise de notoriété internationale (que nous avions pressentie pour une contribution) nous a signalé que la présentation globale du groupe et la publicité des produits individuels relevaient de la «gestion» autonome des directeurs nationaux, et que la maison-mère ne procédait à aucune coordination des marchés. (Seul le nom semble encore venir du pays d'origine.) Une participation au présent ouvrage s'avérait de ce fait impossible.

● Une agence CI de renom international nous a appris que le programme de design développé par elle ne s'appliquait nullement à la publicité, que celle-ci était élaborée par les agences de publicité, indépendamment de l'image développée pour l'entreprise! Nous avons donc dû renoncer à présenter cette étude de cas, malgré l'excellente qualité du travail.

● La brochure de Merck sur la conception graphique dit explicitement: «Dans la publicité moderne des produits, des dérogations créatrices à la conception de base sont possibles et nécessaires.»
Vraiment? Je ne partage nullement ce point de vue. *Car, point n'est alors besoin de lignes directrices dans la conception graphique, inutile de parler de CI* ou de Corporate Design.

2. The design communicative aspect—Corporate Design—shall have priority in this book

● Because the visual effect carries to the outside and really communicates all contents of an identity.

● Because the very design — in reverse also acting towards the inside — contributes to self-comprehension, and helps to create the personality image!

● Because the many chapters on the backgrounds and contexts of a Corporate Design (as a newly created catchword of hopefully profitable effect) do no more than copy banalities from each other.

● Because all of my discoveries and conclusions can only be demonstrated and made clear visually. Abstract and theoretical statements could always be questioned, if not the examples — i.e. the pictures shown — would speak for themselves!

● Because already there are enough books which cover the subject of CI theoretically, without even *hinting at* coherent design processes. What has been missing has been the essential: the presentation of a CI with a matching Corporate Design and its ambiguity.

"Everything that does not happen by accident, happens by design."
(Anonymous)

2. Der gestalterisch-kommunikative Gesichtspunkt – das Corporate Design – soll in diesem Buch den Vorrang haben.

● Weil die visuelle Anmutung jegliche Inhalte einer Identität nach aussen trägt und wirklich vermittelt.

● Weil gerade das Design – umgekehrt auch nach innen wirkend – zum Selbstverständnis beiträgt, das Persönlichkeitsbild sozusagen mitschafft!

● Weil die vielen Episteln über die Hintergründe und Zusammenhänge eines Corporate Design (als neuentdecktes Schlagwort mit erhofft geschäfsträchtiger Wirkung) ohnehin Banalitäten voneinander abschreiben.

● Weil sich alle meine Entdeckungen und Ableitungen nur bildhaft, visuell demonstrieren und veranschaulichen lassen. Abstrakt-theoretische Behauptungen könnten ja jederzeit in Frage gestellt werden, würden nicht die Beispiele – eben die gezeigten Bilder – für sich selbst sprechen!

● Weil es bereits genügend Bücher gibt, die theoretisch das Thema CI abgehandelt haben, ohne auch nur andeutungsweise zusammenhängende Gestaltungsvorgänge *aufzuzeigen*. Das Eigentliche fehlte, die Darstellungsweise einer CI mit einem entsprechenden Corporate Design und die Problematik daraus.

«Alles, was nicht zufällig entsteht, wird gestaltet.» (Anonym)

2. L'aspect communicatif-créatif – le Corporate Design – doit avoir priorité dans le présent ouvrage

● Parce que la représentation visuelle traduit et transmet vers l'extérieur tout contenu d'une identité inhérente.

● Parce que le Design – agissant inversément aussi vers l'intérieur – contribue à la perception de la nature profonde, à la création de la personnalité de l'entreprise!

● Parce que de nombreux traités sur les fondements et implications du Corporate Design (nouvellement découvert et générateur de recettes substantielles) se contentent de copier des banalités les uns sur les autres.

● Parce que toutes mes découvertes et déductions ne peuvent être démontrées et illustrées que visuellement. Toute affirmation théorique abstraite pourrait à tout moment être remise en question si les exemples – donc les images présentées – ne parlaient un langage aussi éloquent!

● Parce qu'il existe déjà suffisamment d'ouvrages qui ont traité théoriquement le thème CI, sans avoir réussi à *exposer* les processus de la création formelle dans toute leur complexité. L'essentiel manquait, la présentation d'une CI avec le Corporate Design correspondant, et les problèmes qui en découlent.

«Tout ce qui ne s'est pas formé par hasard, a été créé.» (Anonyme)

Let us return to the first point:
There is no international Corporate Identity

There may be local CI's. Just as such sometimes intentionally promoted, without any ties to a superimposed concept.
And there are international "brand-identities" (an example here is Coke). The manufacturer only shows Coke: Other products like Sprite, Fanta are added to Coca Cola as independent brands without "company personality". Domitzlaff commented as follows:

"A company represents one brand; two brands are two companies."

I will prove through examples of advertisements in this Introduction that there is no international CI. Look at Pentax in various countries. I will prove it through advertisements for the following reasons:
- because the case studies following in the second part shall demonstrate the *uniformity* of the appearance over a wide area with the other means of communication,
- because for understandable reasons we will not take into consideration TV spots: story boards are a bad replacement for a moving picture,
- because "addy" advertisements best show the fractures in the appearance of a company.
Because Corporate Identity obviously stops, where advertising comes in.
CD, however, the way I see it, is not l'art pour l'art, is not self-purpose.
"What a miracle it is, if a manufacturer succeeds in finding for his advertising a style which lasts for many years. A certain courage, too, will then be required to *remain* with it."
(Dr. Fritz Eichler)

Kehren wir zu der ersten Behauptung zurück:
Es gibt keine internationale Corporate Identity

Es gibt vielleicht lokale CIs. Manchmal gerade als solche bewusst gefördert, ohne Anbindung an ein übergeordnetes Konzept.
Und es gibt internationale «brand identities» (ein Beispiel wäre Coke). Der Hersteller tritt mit Coca-Cola in Erscheinung. Dazu kommen andere, Sprite, Fanta, als eigenständige Marken ohne «company personality». Domitzlaff sagte dazu:

«Eine Firma hat eine Marke, zwei Marken sind zwei Firmen.»

Ich werde mit den Anzeigenbeispielen dieses Vorworts beweisen, dass es keine internationale CI gibt. (Schauen Sie Pentax aus verschiedenen Ländern an.) Ich werde es deshalb vorwiegend mit Anzeigen tun,
- weil die im zweiten Teil folgenden «case studies» die *Geschlossenheit* des Auftritts über einen breiteren Bereich mit den übrigen Kommunikationsmitteln vorstellen sollen,
- weil wir das Medium TV-Spot aus verständlichen Gründen unberücksichtigt lassen («storyboards» sind ein schlechter Ersatz für ein bewegtes Bild),
- weil sich mit den Werbeaufmachungen am ehesten die Brüche im Erscheinungsbild eines Unternehmens erkennen lassen.
Denn Corporate Identity hört offenbar immer auf, wenn es zur Werbung kommt.
Das entsprechende CD aber, so wie ich es verstehe, ist nicht l'art pour l'art, ist nicht Selbstzweck.
«Was für ein Wunder ist es doch, wenn es einem Produzenten gelingt, für seine Werbung einen eindrucksvollen Stil zu finden, der viele Jahre hält. Es bedarf dann aber auch eines gewissen Mutes, dabei zu *bleiben*.»
(Dr. Fritz Eichler)

Revenons à la première affirmation:
Il n'existe pas de Corporate Identity internationale

Il existe peut-être des CI locales. Quelques-une font l'objet d'une promotion précisément comme telles, sans rapport avec un concept global.
Et il y a des «brand-identities» internationales (exemple: Coke) où le producteur se présente sous la marque Coca Cola. Citons aussi les cas de Sprite ou Fanta, commes marques sans «company personality». Domitzlaff écrit à ce sujet:

«Une entreprise a une marque, deux marques sont deux entreprises.»

Au moyen d'exemples de la publicité-presse, je prouverai qu'il n'existe pas de CI internationale. Regardez Pentax dans les différents pays. A l'appui de ma thèse, je citerai primairement des annonces:
- parce que les études de cas exposées dans la seconde partie ont pour but de montrer *l'unité* et *la cohérence* dans la présentation de l'entreprise avec ses divers secteurs, en utilisant les autres médias de communication,
- parce que, pour des raisons évidentes, le spot télévisé n'est pas pris en considération comme média: les «storyboards» remplacent difficilement l'image animée,
- parce que les présentations publicitaires sont particulièrement révélatrices des failles dans la CI. Car la Corporate Identity semble s'arrêter là où intervient la publicité.
Le CD correspondant, tel que je le conçois, n'est cependant pas de l'art pour l'art, ni une fin en soi.
«Cela touche presque au miracle lorsqu'un producteur réussit à trouver pour sa publicité un style percutant qui reste valable pendant des années. Il faut cependant aussi un certain courage pour *maintenir* ce style.»
(Fritz Eichler)

Some Japanese have shown us in Europe with persistence and *long-term thinking* and at largest possible business success what a consistent CI is worth; although on the other hand, Japanese companies present themselves with the usual CD errors in the United States (because, it appears, they listen too much to smart "Ad" managers).

Nevertheless, some Japanese brands have a "personality", a CD, a relative uniform appearance of high quality, of which quite a few large American and German firms can only dream.

In my experience, no firm can have a rounded company CI, if it practices the American "Product Management System" characterized by its delegated individual responsibilities, which are used particularly in advertising.

Even at assumed CI intentions of top management, the "superimposed concept" will daily necessarily be dissolved by the individual product manager. CI is bound to fail at the criteria the "PM" is evaluated by: *His* personal proof of success, his "profit contribution", his accrued company earnings. No matter, *how he* made it! Whether with, without or even against a CI. The main thing is that "his" campaign has brought sales and increased profits! No matter, what happens later.

There will also be no "company personality" in the meaning of my explanations in eastern oriented countries. And what for? Competition and thus the required exposition and personalization are not needed in a planned economy.

Einige Japaner haben uns in Europa mit Beharrlichkeit und *Langfristdenken* mit grösstem Geschäftserfolg vorgemacht, was eine konsequente CI wert ist. Obwohl gleichzeitig japanische Firmenpräsentation in Amerika mit den üblichen CD-Fehlern aufwartet (weil vielleicht zu sehr auf gewiefte «Ad»-Manager gehört wurde).

Immerhin haben einige japanische Marken eine «personality», ein CD, ein relativ einheitlich qualitätvolles Bild, von dem mancher US-Konzern und manche europäische Firma nur träumen kann.

Es kann nach meiner Erfahrung bei keinem Unternehmen eine geschlossene Firmen-CI geben, solange das amerikanische «Product-Management-System» mit seiner delegierten Einzelverantwortung gerade bei der Werbung praktiziert wird.

Selbst bei unterstellten CI-Absichten des Top-Managements wird tagtäglich das «übergeordnete Konzept» durch den einzelnen Produktmanager aufgelöst werden müssen. CI muss scheitern an dem, woran der «PM» gemessen wird:

Seinem persönlichen Erfolgsnachweis, seiner «profit contribution», seinem gescheffelten Gewinn. Gleichgültig, *wie er* das geschafft hat! Ob mit, ohne oder gar gegen eine CI. Hauptsache, «seine» Kampagne hat Umsatz gemacht und den Profit vergrössert! Egal, was nachher kommt.

Es wird auch keine «Firmenpersönlichkeit» im Sinne meiner Ausführungen in östlich orientierten Ländern geben. Wozu auch? Ein Wettbewerb und somit notwendige Alleinstellung und Profilierung wird bei einer Planwirtschaft nicht gebraucht.

Certains Japonais – dont la réussite commerciale est impressionnante – nous ont démontré, en Europe, les mérites d'une CI systématique, réalisée avec persévérance et une *conception à long terme*. N'empêche que, parallèlement, la présentation des entreprises japonaises en Amérique est entachée des erreurs CD habituelles (peut-être pour avoir écouté des «ad-managers» trop roués).

Quoiqu'il en soit, certaines marques japonaises ont une «personality», un CD, une image qualitative relativement homogène, dont maint groupe industriel aux Etats-Unis et mainte société européenne ne peuvent que rêver.

Aucune CI intégrale ne saurait exister aussi longtemps que le système américain du «Product Management», avec son principe de la responsabilité individuelle déléguée, est pratiqué précisément au niveau de la publicité. Même lorsque la Direction générale a des intentions CI bien définies, la CI échoue inévitablement devant les critères mesurant la prestation du «Product Manager», à savoir *son* succès personnel, sa «profit contribution». Peu importe *comment il* a réussi! Avec, sans ou même contre une CI. L'essentiel est que «sa» campagne ait augmenté le chiffre d'affaires et ait rapporté gros!

La «personnalité d'entreprise» au sens de mes considérations précédentes me paraît également exclue pour les pays de l'Est. A quoi servirait-elle? La compétition et, partant, la nécessité de se profiler par rapport aux autres, n'a plus de sens dans une économie dirigée.

11

Almost all examples in the Introduction are thus rather "denunciations", even if they are only representative and really accidental (!), standing for hundreds of others.

The companies as such are not really meant, the company names are interchangeable, because we can show the same mistakes *all over* — even with firms, which are repeatedly cited as good examples for a successful CI, like even IBM or such "ideal examples" from my earlier books.

After working at this book, I must say: many known images may not even be called by that name. They are rather graphic in-house prints — standardizations and car park labellings.

Almost all Corporate Designs are vulnerable or questionable at one point or another.

● Because e.g. a DC designer really represents himself, the company personality disappears behind his designs and arrangements.

In a CI *everything* has to be in conformity: the offer and the design. Above all there has to be continuity and congruity from performance to communication.

There must be dependability and reliability. An advertising campaign which has impact and which is "promising" and spectacular, *does by no means need to be efficient.*

Even if the known saying of Bernbach is: "Good advertising kills a bad product faster", this can be turned around, if one says: "A good product cannot even be killed by bad advertising."

Fast alle Beispiele im Vorwort sind somit eher «Anprangerungen», wenn sie auch nur stellvertretend und wirklich zufällig (!) für hundert andere stehen. Die Unternehmen sind als solche gar nicht gemeint, die Firmennamen sind austauschbar, weil wir die gleichen Fehler *überall* aufzeigen können – auch bei solchen Firmen, die immer wieder als gute Beispiele für eine gelungene CI herangezogen werden, wie selbst IBM oder jene «Vorbilder» aus meinen früheren Büchern.

Ich muss nach der Arbeit an diesem Buch feststellen: Viele bekannte Erscheinungsbilder dürften gar nicht so heissen. Es sind eher grafische Hausdrucksachen – Normierungen und Fahrzeugbeschriftungen.

Fast alle Corporate Designs sind an der einen oder anderen Stelle angreifbar, fragwürdig.

● Weil zum Beispiel ein CD-Designer eigentlich sich selbst profiliert. Die Persönlichkeit des Unternehmens verschwindet hinter seinen Entwürfen und Reglementen.

Es muss bei einer CI *alles* übereinstimmen: das Angebot und die Darstellung. Es muss vor allem Kontinuität geben und Kongruenz von Leistung zur Kommunikation.

Es muss Verlässlichkeit und Zuverlässigkeit geben. Eine Werbekampagne, die sogenannten Impact hat, die «vielversprechend» und auffällig ist, *braucht noch lange nicht verkaufswirksam zu sein.*

Wenn der bekannte Spruch von Bernbach auch heisst:
«Gute Werbung tötet ein schlechtes Produkt schneller», so kann man ihn auch umdrehen und sagen: «Ein gutes Produkt kann nicht einmal durch schlechte Werbung getötet werden.»

Presque tous les exemples cités dans l'avant-propos sont donc plutôt des CD «mis au pilori»: pourtant, leur choix a été totalement aléatoire (!) et ils sont simplement représentatifs de centaines d'autres. Les entreprises ne sont pas visées en tant que telles, car les mêmes erreurs se reproduisent *partout* – même dans les entreprises souvent citées à titre d'exemple pour leur CI réussi, comme par exemple IBM ou les «modèles» que j'ai proposés dans mes ouvrages antérieurs.

Après étude de la vaste documentation pour le présent ouvrage, je dois constater que beaucoup d'identités d'entreprise ne méritent pas ce nom.

Presque tous les Corporate Design sont contestables, problématiques en un point ou l'autre.

Parce que, par exemple, un créateur CD entend se profiler lui-même. La personnalité de l'entreprise s'estompe derrière ses projets et règlements.

Dans une CI, *tout* doit concorder: l'offre et sa présentation. Elle doit avant tout respecter la continuité et la congruence entre performances et communication.

Elle doit inspirer sécurité et confiance. Une campagne publicitaire qui a de l'«impact», qui est «prometteuse» et percutante, *ne se traduit pas nécessairement par de meilleures ventes.*

Si la célèbre maxime de Bernbach affirme qu'«une bonne publicité tue un mauvais produit plus rapidement», il suffit de l'inverser pour dire: «Un bon produit ne peut même pas être tué par une mauvaise publicité.»

Het beste is niet noodzakelijk het duurste en het ingewikkeldste.

IBM

Suzuki hat drei traurige Neuigkeiten für alle Ölscheichs.

ANZEIGE

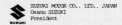

Ever so often in marketing circles I hear the intentional claim of the importance of a unified appearance. Successful companies which don't even want a CI, but only have product brands, are then cited.

Admittedly: in most cases the average reader with little or no interest skims through what occupies us "experts" in such detail. The only proof is in what has been sold. *That* for the advertising man and marketing executive is the alibi for "stubborness" and uncompromising independence.

The customer, so it is argued, is for instance totally indifferent as to which typeface the company uses, whether it is changed or whether the logo is consistently used; he would not even notice.

I don't believe this: Prof. Theuer said: "The short-term pleasant usually creates the long-term damageable." Therefore, what do we want to reach by a consistent design philosophy? By the claim for homogenousness? By *uniformity?* (as "Creative Art Directors" say derogatively).

The first answer is:
Economy! We wish to work more efficiently. We wish to cumulate effects. When a new product (or offer) enters a market, it needs a minimum of advertising money in order to win at all!

Experience shows that this expenditure is up to ten times higher, if something totally unknown is concerned. If however, the producer already has a name — possibly even an image of quality (!) — confidence and recognition create a solid platform.

Ich höre immer wieder in Marketing-kreisen die Zweckbehauptung von der Belanglosigkeit eines einheitlichen Auftretens. Man zitiert dann geschäftlich erfolgreiche Firmen, die gar keine CI wollen, sondern nur Produktmarken haben.

Zugegeben: Meist überblättert der Durchschnittskunde uninteressiert das, was uns «Experten» im Detail so beschäftigt. Als einziger Beleg gilt, dass gekauft wird. *Das* ist für Werbemacher und Marketing-Verantwortliche das Alibi für «Eigensinn» und kompromisslose Unabhängigkeit.

Dem Kunden, so das Argument, sei zum Beispiel völlig gleichgültig, welche Schrift die Firma einsetzt, ob gewechselt wird oder ob das Zeichen kontinuierlich verwendet ist, er merke es nicht einmal.

Ich glaube das nicht. Prof. Theuer hat gesagt: «Kurzfristig Angenehmes erzeugt im Regelfall langfristig Schädigendes.» Ergo: Was wollen wir erreichen mit konformer Gestaltungsphilosophie? Der Forderung nach Einheitlichkeit? Mit *Uniformität?* (Wie «Creative Art Directors» abwertend sagen.)

Die erste Antwort heisst:
Ökonomie! Wir wollen effizienter arbeiten. Wir wollen Wirkung kumulieren.

Wenn ein neues Produkt (oder Angebot) auf den Markt kommt, braucht es ein Minimum an Werbegeld, um sich überhaupt durchzusetzen! Dieser Einsatz ist nachweislich bis zu zehnmal höher, wenn etwas Unbekanntes auftaucht. Hat jedoch der Hersteller schon einen Namen – womöglich noch ein Image von Qualität (!) –, so schaffen Vertrauen und Wiedererkennung eine solide Plattform.

Dans les milieux du marketing, l'idée de la futilité d'une présentation cohérente est largement répandue. Et l'on cite même des entreprises travaillant avec succès, tout en refusant d'avoir une CI et en se contentant de marques de produits.

Certes: le plus souvent le client moyen feuillette sans grand intérêt ce qui passionne l'«expert» jusque dans le détail. La seule chose qui compte, c'est la conclusion de l'acte d'achat. Pour le publicitaire et le responsable du marketing, c'est là l'alibi qui justifie son «obstination», son indépendance au-dessus de tout compromis.

Le client, argumente-t-on, reste par exemple indifférent au type de caractères utilisés par l'entreprise, aux changements ou à la continuité d'usage d'un signe, il ne remarque même pas la différence.

Je ne crois pas que cela soit vrai. Le professeur Theuer a dit: «L'agrément à court terme produit en règle générale le désagrément à long terme.» Alors, que voulons-nous atteindre par une philosophie de la création visuelle? Par l'exigence de cohérence? Par l'*uniformité?* (Comme disent les «Creative Art directors», avec une note péjorative.)

La première réponse sera:
Economie! Nous voulons travailler plus efficacement. Nous voulons réaliser un effet cumulatif.

Lorsqu'un nouveau produit (ou une nouvelle offre) est lancé sur le marché, il faut un minimum de fonds publicitaires pour pouvoir s'imposer! L'expérience prouve que le montant est jusqu'à dix fois plus élevé lorsqu'il s'agit de quelque chose d'inconnu. Toutefois, si le producteur a déjà un nom – s'il a même une image de qualité (!) – la confiance et la réminiscence créent une plateforme solide.

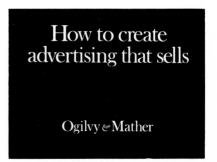

How to create advertising that sells

Ogilvy & Mather

The second answer is:

Significance, profile and exposition! For years and years I have been collecting advertisements, logos, and the pertaining "rhymes" of the entrepreneurs.

Hundreds of them are filling my library. In this Introduction I will demonstrate the symptomatic aspects using a few examples and comparing them. Moreover, a little later I will show twelve brief counter-examples, which prove the disadvantages of a missing company profile and company appearance.

I am doing this to demonstrate the uneconomical advertising nonsense of bi-annual and campaign thinking, which wastes millions of company communication funds. Those soap and detergent companies, which have enough money, may continue to proceed in such a way in the future. However, I will try to let you, dear reader, see the CI interest moneys, which can be earned from uniform design. "For products and services, which at similar prices are almost equal, the consumer decides according to the so-called psychological additional benefit, which presents itself in design, form, color, typeface, image and argumentation."
(Dietmar Gottschall)

The prerequisite is an individual, significant and above all recognizable picture.

However, to say one thing in advance — and to anticipate my critics:
I don't think anything of merely graphically oriented, system-dominated and thus stupid design manuals.

Die zweite Antwort heisst:

Signifikanz, Profil und Alleinstellung! Ich habe über Jahre hinweg Anzeigen gesammelt, Firmenzeichen und dazugehörende «Sprüche» der Unternehmen.

Hunderte füllen mein Archiv. Ich zeige in diesem Vorwort anhand einiger weniger Beispiele und durch Gegenüberstellung Symptomatisches auf. Ausserdem will ich etwas später mit zwölf knappen Gegenbeispielen versuchen, die Nachteile eines fehlenden Firmenprofils und Unternehmensauftritts zu belegen.

Ich will damit den unökonomischen Reklameunsinn von Halbjahres- und Kampagnedenken vorführen, womit Millionen an Firmenkommunikationsgeldern verplempert werden. Jene Seifen- und Waschmittelfirmen, die über genug Geld verfügen, mögen auch ferner so verfahren. Aber ich werde versuchen, Sie, liebe Leser, die CI-Zinsen sehen zu lassen, die eine geschlossene Gestaltung einbringt. «Bei Produkten und Leistungen, die bei ähnlichen Preisen nahezu gleich sind, entscheidet der Konsument nach dem sogenannten psychologischen Zusatznutzen, der sich im Design, in Form, Farbe, Schrift, Bild und Argumentation präsentiert.»
(Dietmar Gottschall)

Voraussetzung ist ein eigenständiges, signifikantes und vor allem wiedererkennbares Bild.

Um aber eines gleich vorweg zu sagen – und um es meinen Kritikern aus der Hand zu nehmen:
Ich halte überhaupt nichts von rein grafisch orientierten, systemreglementierenden und damit stupiden Gestaltungshandbüchern.

La deuxième réponse sera:

Traits caractéristiques, profil et image saillante!
Pendant des années, j'ai collectionné des annonces, des symboles d'entreprise et les slogans correspondants. Mes archives contiennent des centaines d'exemples. Quelques-uns suffiront pour révéler, par simple comparaison, les symptômes les plus marquants.

A l'aide de douze exemples «négatifs», j'essaierai d'expliquer quels sont les préjudices produits par l'absence de profil ou d'identité cohérente d'une entreprise.

Ce faisant, je me propose de démontrer le non-sens et l'aberration économique de conceptions axées sur la promotion publicitaire semestrielle et les campagnes publicitaires, où les fonds destinés à la communication visuelle de l'entreprise sont dilapidés par millions. Je préfère, cher lecteur, dégager pour vous les «intérêts» CI que produit une création formelle harmonieuse.
«En présence de produits et de performances semblables, offerts à des prix quasiment identiques, c'est le consommateur qui décide en fonction de «l'effet psychologique additionnel», qui s'exprime par le design, la forme, la couleur, les caractères d'impression, l'image et l'argumentation.»
(Dietmar Gottschall)

La condition à remplir est une image spécifique, saillante et, surtout, facilement reconnaissable.

Mais, je dois dire d'emblée (pour éviter à mes détracteurs de devoir intervenir) que je m'inscris en faux contre les affirmations des stupides manuels sur l'art visuel, orientés uniquement vers la création graphique ou la réglementation systématique.

There is much to do.
Let's get at it. Esso
We like to help: yours AEG
Shell. We help you keep going.
VW. There you know what you get.
Persil — there you know what you get

Es gibt viel zu tun. Packen wir's an.

Wir helfen gern: Ihre AEG

Shell. Wir helfen Ihnen weiter.

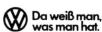 Da weiß man, was man hat.

Persil-da weiss man, was man hat

Il y a beaucoup à faire.
Commençons avec énergie. Esso.
Nous vous aidons volontiers:
votre AEG
Shell. Nous vous aidons à aller plus loin.
VW. On sait ce qu'on a.
Persil – on sait ce qu'on a.

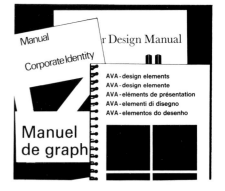

Standardizing, narrowing, prescribing and *prohibiting*—this will only create resistance on the marketing side and with Art Directors, as they would fear for their freedom of "creativity".
I have always seen more sense in *inspiring,* and even *exciting* and primarily also in *comparing* examples (positive and negative).
And this is how I should like to see this book understood! *None* of the examples judged negatively should insult the originator as ridiculed.
If you, dear unaffected reader, will smile once in a while, please consider: it could perhaps have been you, whose work was shown.

As, after all, we, the others, the non-concerned always know better anyway.

Is not that so?

Before showing the advertising design pictures mentioned earlier, I would like to name the CI criteria. This appears to me as a necessary task, as in this book I am primarily dealing with the CD aspect, and we have to be aware of the fact that this is only one of the CI elements, even if possibly the most important one.

Normieren, einengen, vorschreiben und *verbieten* – damit wird nur Widerstand auf Marketingseite und bei Art Directors erzeugt, da sie um ihren Freiraum für «Kreativität» fürchten.
Ich habe immer mehr Sinn darin gesehen, mit Beispielen (positiven wie negativen) *anzuregen,* sogar *aufzuregen* und, vor allem aber, zu *vergleichen.*
Und so möchte ich dieses Buch verstanden wissen! *Keines* der als negativ empfundenen Beispiele soll den Urheber besserwisserisch blessieren. Wenn Sie, unbetroffener Leser, manchmal schmunzeln mögen, bedenken Sie: Es hätten vielleicht auch Sie sein können, dessen Arbeiten abgebildet sind.

Denn schliesslich wissen wir anderen, Unbeteiligten, es sowieso immer besser.

Nicht wahr?

Vor die erwähnten gestalterisch-werblichen Bildseiten will ich aber zuerst die CI-Kriterien stellen.
Das scheint mir eine notwendige Pflichtübung, da ich mich in diesem Buch vorwiegend mit dem CD-Aspekt abgebe und wir uns bewusst sein müssen, dass dies eben nur eines der CI-Elemente ist, wenn auch vielleicht das tragendste.

Normalisation, restriction, prescription et *interdiction* = mesures suscitant la réticence des spécialistes du marketing et des directeurs d'art qui craignent de perdre la liberté nécessaire à leur «créativité».
Il me semble plus valable, par des exemples (positifs et négatifs), d'*inciter* à l'action, voire même d'*exciter* pour stimuler à la *réaction* et, surtout, à la *comparaison.*
C'est ainsi que j'aimerais voir compris ce livre! Aucun des exemples considérés comme négatifs ne doit blesser l'auteur dans son amour-propre.
Si parfois, n'étant pas directement concerné, vous avez envie de sourire, cher ami lecteur, n'oubliez pas que vos travaux pourraient tout aussi bien être reproduits ci-contre.

Car nous autres, qui sommes «au-dessus de la mêlée», nous sommes toujours meilleurs que les autres.

N'est-ce pas?

Les pages illustrées, présentant les créations de l'art visuel et publicitaire, seront précédées des critères CI. Cet exercice s'impose, étant donné que ce livre est consacré primairement à l'aspect CD et que nous devons reconnaître que ce n'est là qu'un élément CI parmi d'autres, même s'il s'avère être éventuellement l'élément sustentateur par excellence.

15

Elements of Corporate Identity

as already generally discussed, here newly subdivided and supplemented

Elemente der Corporate Identity

wie sie allgemein schon diskutiert, hier neu geordnet und ergänzt sind

Eléments de la Corporate Identity

déjà discutés de manière générale, reclassés et complétés ici:

I. Corporate Identity

1. Name
- Addition to name
- Appearance of name

2. Background
- The historical grown
- Self-comprehension

3. Definition of Goal
- e.g. diversification
- modification, etc.

II. Company Conduct

1. Product and Service Offer
- Quality, safety, reliability
- Intruistic or economic value
- Price/performance relationship
- Serviceability

2. Sales Concept
- Trade relationships
- Consumer relationships

3. External Divisions
- Sales representatives
- Display service
- Customer service (repairs, complaints, etc.)

4. Financial Management

5. Personnel Policies
(Feeling of belonging: pride!)
- Salary, social benefits, contracts, evaluation, reward, congratulation forms, "gold needle", etc.
- Staff assembly
- Training program, advanced education, seminary, etc.
- Fringe benefits, company car, discount buying, company resorts, etc.
- System of staff-suggested improvements
- Department designation
- Black board, etc.

I. Unternehmens-Identität

1. Name
- Zusatz zum Namen
- Bild des Namens

2. Hintergrund
- historisch Gewachsenes
- Selbstverständnis

3. Zieldefinition
- z. B. Diversifikation
- Veränderung usw.

II. Unternehmens-Verhalten

1. Produkt oder Serviceangebot
- Qualität, Sicherheit, Zuverlässigkeit
- Gebrauchs- oder Nutzungswert
- Preis/Leistungs-Verhältnis
- Servicefreundlichkeit

2. Vertriebskonzeption
- Handelsbeziehungen
- Konsumentenbeziehungen

3. Aussendienste
- Vertreter
- Dekorationsdienst
- Kundendienst (Reparatur, Reklamation) usw.

4. Finanzmanagement

5. Personalpolitik
(Zugehörigkeitsgefühl: Stolz!)
- Gehalt, Soziales, Verträge, Zeugnis, Urkunde, Auszeichnung, Glückwunsch, «Goldene Nadel» usw.
- Betriebsversammlung
- Schulungsprogramm, Weiterbildungsseminar usw.
- Vergünstigungen («fringe benefits»)
  Firmenwagen, verbilligter Einkauf, Firmenkurheime usw.
- Vorschlagswesen
- Abteilungsbezeichnung
- Schwarzes Brett usw.

I. Identité de l'entreprise

1. Raison sociale
- Adjonction à la raison sociale
- Symbole de la raison sociale

2. Arrière-plan
- Données historiques
- L'entreprise vue par elle-même

3. Définition des objectifs
- p. ex. diversification
- changement, etc.

II. Comportement de l'entreprise

1. Offre de produits ou de services
- Qualité, sécurité, fiabilité
- Valeur d'usage/Valeur utile
- Rapport prix/rendement
- Qualité du service

2. Conception de la distribution
- Relations commerciales
- Relations avec les consommateurs

3. Services extérieurs
- Agents
- Service de décoration
- Service après-vente (réparations, réclamations), etc.

4. Gestion financière

5. Politique du personnel
(esprit de famille: fierté!)
- Rémunération, questions sociales, contrats, certificats, attestations, distinctions, félicitations, «épingle d'or», etc.
- Assemblée d'entreprise
- Programme de formation, séminaire de perfectionnement, etc.
- Avantages spéciaux («fringe benefits»), voiture d'entreprise, achats au rabais, maison de repos de l'entreprise, etc.
- Système de propositions
- Désignation des différents services
- Tableau d'affichage, etc.

III. Company Appearance

1. Guideline
- Design Manual, company philosophy
- Organizational brochure

2. Brand
- Signet, symbol
- Logo

3. Design / Identification Features
- Company colors, color system
- Typographic principles, typeface
- Principles of material selection
- Language, language adjustments
- Selection principles for media
- Design principles

IV. Company Communication

1. External Communication
- Advertising
  TV spot, film, radio spot
  slide video show
  product/service advertisement
  image advertising (also personnel ad and balance sheet publication)
  poster
  brochure, catalogue, leaflet
  packaging
  display material, window sticker
  external advertising
  direct mail, etc.
- Annual Report

2. Public Relations / Publicity Work
- Communal conduct
- Newspaper articles, television reports
- Environmental factors
- General correspondence
- Telephone answering, greetings
- Entry in telephone books and Yellow Pages

3. Internal Communication
- Internal memo, organizational chart, report, form, stamp, etc.
- company/in-house bulletin

III. Unternehmens-Erscheinungsbild

1. Leitbild
- Design Manual, Firmenphilosophie
- Organisationsbroschüre

2. Marke
- Signet, Zeichen
- Logotype

3. Gestaltungs-/Identifikationsmerkmale
- Hausfarbe, Farbsystem
- Typografische Prinzipien, Schriftart
- Prinzipien der Materialauswahl
- Sprache, Sprachregelungen
- Selektionsprinzipien für Medien
- Gestaltungsprinzipien

IV. Unternehmens-Kommunikation

1. Externe Kommunikation
- Werbung
  TV-Spot, Film, Dia-Tonbildschau
  Rundfunkspot
  Produkt-/Serviceanzeige
  Imagewerbung (auch Personalanzeige und Bilanzveröffentlichung)
  Plakat
  Broschüre, Katalog, Prospekt
  Verpackung
  Displaymaterial, Fensterkleber
  Aussenwerbung, Direct Mail usw.
- Geschäftsbericht

2. Public Relations/Öffentlichkeitsarbeit
- Kommunalverhalten
- Zeitungsartikel, Fernsehberichte
- Umweltbewusstsein
- Allgemeine Korrespondenz
- Telefonmeldung, Begrüssung
- Eintrag in Branchen- und Telefonbüchern

3. Interne Kommunikation
- Hausmitteilung, Organisationsverfügung, Bericht, Formular, Stempel usw.
- Betriebs-/Hauszeitschrift

III. Image de l'entreprise

1. Concept directeur
- Manuel de design, philosophie de l'entreprise
- Brochure d'organisation

2. Marque
- Sigle, signe
- Logotype

3. Conception/identification
- Les couleurs
- La typographie
- Le choix du matériel
- Les langues
- Les médias
- Principes de conception

IV. Communication de l'entreprise

1. Communication externe
- Publicité
  spot TV et radio, film,
  présentation audiovisuelle
  annonce (produit, service)
  l'image de l'entreprise (publications relatives au personnel, au bilan)
  affiche
  brochure, catalogue, prospectus
  conditionnement
  display, vitrine
  publicité extérieure
  publicité directe (direct mail)
- Rapport d'exercice

2. Relations publiques
- RP sur le plan communal
- Articles de journaux, reportages
- Facteurs écologiques
- Correspondance générale
- Service téléphonique, accueil
- Inscription dans l'annuaire téléphonique et le répertoire par branches

3. Communication interne
- Informations, organisation, rapport, formulaire, cachet, etc.
- Bulletin d'information, journal

4. Printed Matters / Miscellaneous

- Printed matters, letterhead, normal envelope, large envelope sticker, form, invoice, agreement, order confirmation, information, circular, calling card, recommendation, proposal folder, sales rep. folder, etc.
- Special branch-related requirements (e.g. with banks) statement of account, savings book cheque card, check book, etc.
- Material accompanying product (e.g. for hardware producers) operating instructions warranty card shipping papers, etc.
- Advertising presents
- Fairs, exhibitions
- Speech, symposium (Share holders assembly)
- Uniforms name sign

5. Architecture (Building-, Headoffice and Subsidiary Designation)

- Reception, meeting room
- Office
- Manufacturing facilities
- Casino, cafeteria, washing rooms
- Orientation elements (color orientation system, orientation signs)
- Company signs, etc.

6. Vehicles

- Brand: prestige!
- Painting, labelling

In the following part, this book will only deal with Corporate Design, the advertising aspect and communication.

4. Hausdrucksachen/ Verschiedenes

- Geschäftsdrucksachen Briefpapier, Briefumschlag, Versandhülle, Aufkleber, Formular, Rechnung, Vertrag, Auftragsbestätigung Information, Rundschreiben Visitenkarte, Empfehlung Angebotsmappe, Vertreterfolder usw.
- Spezielle branchenbezogene Erfordernisse (z.B. bei Banken) Sparbuch Kontoauszug Scheckkarte, Scheckbuch usw.
- Produktbegleitendes Material (z.B. bei Hardware-Produzenten) Gebrauchsanleitung Garantiekarte Versandpapiere usw.
- Werbegeschenke
- Messe, Ausstellung
- Vortrag, Veranstaltung (Aktionärsversammlung)
- «Dienst»-Kleidung Namensschild

5. Architektur (Gebäude-, Firmen- und Filialkennzeichnung)

- Rezeption, Besprechungsraum
- Büro
- Fertigungsstätten
- Kasino, Kantine, Waschräume
- Orientierungselemente (Farbleitsystem, Hinweisschilder)
- Firmenschilder usw.

6. Fahrzeuge

- Marke: Prestige!
- Bemalung, Beschriftung

Dieses Buch wird sich im folgenden Teil nur noch mit dem Corporate Design, dem werblichen Aspekt und der Kommunikation auseinandersetzen.

4. Imprimés d'entreprise/ divers

- Imprimés commerciaux papier à lettre, enveloppe, bande d'envoi, étiquette, formulaire, facture, contrat, confirmation de la commande information, circulaire, carte de visite, de vœux, recueil d'offres, portefeuille de représentant, etc.
- Exigences spécifiques à une branche (p. ex. banques) livret d'épargne extrait de compte chèques: carte, carnet, etc.
- Documents accompagnant les produits (pour producteurs de matériel) mode d'emploi carte de garantie documents d'expédition, etc.
- Cadeaux publicitaires
- Foires, expositions
- Conférence, manifestation spéciale (assemblée des actionnaires)
- Uniformes plaquette nominative, «badge»

5. Architecture (identification des bâtiments, sociétés, succursales)

- Réception, salle de conférence
- Bureau
- Ateliers de production
- Casino, cantine, salles d'eau
- Eléments d'orientation (couleurs, panneaux indicateurs)
- Enseignes, etc.

6. Véhicules

- Marque: prestige!
- Couleurs, inscriptions

Dans la suite, le présent ouvrage se concentrera uniquement sur le Corporate Design, l'aspect publicitaire et la communication.

What visual features lead to a uniform "identity" or a consistent "personality"?

Welche visuellen Merkmale machen eine geschlossene «Identity» oder durchgängige «Personality» aus?

Quels sont les critères visuels déterminants d'une «identité» cohérente ou d'une «personnalité» intégrale?

Seven basic rules for the design (the CD) within a Corporate Identity

Sieben Grundregeln für die Gestaltung (das CD) im Rahmen einer Corporate Identity

Sept règles fondamentales de l'art visuel (le CD) dans le cadre d'une Corporate Identity

(1) (2) (3)

1 Advertisement of the Swedish advertising agency Erlandson & Falck
2 Volvo advertisement in the daily newspaper "Welt"
3 Advertisement for German wine
4 Elevenfold change of company logo in forty-seven years

1 Anzeige der schwedischen Werbeagentur (Erlandson & Falck)
2 Volvo-Anzeige in der Tageszeitung «Welt»
3 Werbung für deutschen Wein
4 Elfmaliger Wechsel des Firmenzeichens in siebenundvierzig Jahren

1 Annonce de l'agence de publicité suédoise Erlandson & Falck
2 Annonce Volvo dans le quotidien «Welt»
3 Publicité pour un vin allemand
4 Changement du symbole d'entreprise à onze reprises en l'espace de 47 ans

Rule 1
Brand and design appearance must be in conformity (style, appearance).
● Statement and visual demonstration must correspond to each other.
● Overall expression, visual quality must suit image.

Rule 2
Design elements must be clearly and unequivocally defined and must be maintained in the long run:
● Overall effect, styling means
● Company sign, logo type
● Company typeface (typographic order)
● Company colors
Changes following fashionable trends of the time, or to "tendentiously" meet with people's taste, cause confusion and cost effort, money and time: *in order to create a new, strange appearance!*

Regel 1
Marke und gestalterischer Auftritt müssen übereinstimmen (Stil, Erscheinungsbild).
● Aussage und entsprechende visuelle Ausformung müssen sich entsprechen.
● Gesamtausdruck, visuelle Qualität müssen zum Image passen.

Regel 2
Gestaltungselemente sind klar und eindeutig festzulegen und dann auch langfristig durchzuhalten:
● Gesamtanmutung, stilbildende Mittel
● Firmenzeichen, Schriftzug
● Hausschrift (typografische Ordnung)
● Hausfarben
Wechselspiele, modisch-typografischer Zeitgeschmäcklerei folgend oder um «trendgerecht» dem sogenannten Publikumsgeschmack zu entsprechen, erzeugen Verwirrung, kosten Anstrengungen, Geld und Zeit: *um ein neues, fremdes Bild zu schaffen!*

1re règle
La marque et la présentation formelle doivent concorder (style, image d'identification)
● Le texte et la conception visuelle correspondante doivent harmoniser.
● L'impression d'ensemble et la qualité visuelle doivent cadrer avec l'image.

2e règle
Les éléments de la conception visuelle doivent être définis avec clarté et précision, puis maintenus à long terme:
● présentation globale, moyens d'effet stylistique
● symbole d'entreprise, logotype
● bulletin d'entreprise (disposition typographique)
● couleurs d'entreprise
Les fréquents changements, en fonction de la «mode» typographique ou des goûts momentanés, sèment la confusion et coûtent des efforts, de l'argent et du temps: *pour aboutir à une image nouvelle, parfaitement inconnue!*

(4)

Rule 3

All design factors and design criteria must have the possibility of being transferrable from one medium to the other and must be applied uniformly.

The elements of a company appearance must be recognizably visible in every form of company presentation.

The opposite page shows a reproduction which I have been permitted to take from Volume I of "Basic Design Elements and Their Systems", CoCoMAS Committee.

This illustration uses the "Mazda tree" to very vividly show, how the individual design factors spreading to all areas of company presentation can convey a uniform appearance of a company:

The typefaces are clearly defined: in the upper block of the corporate logo type, there are predominantly ideograms in "kanji", i.e. word formations. In the second block of the vehicle labelling we read "katakana", a syllable typeface, which formally matches the Latin alphabet underneath. (Important for export!)

Opel Germany is in (purposeful!) contrast to the above. Every car model has a different individual labelling — not only in the rear — and again different in the advertisements.

The right-hand advertisement for instance in copy has a different Manta typeface than that on the car sign, and above the advertisement we have placed the label that we saw on the trunk of the car.

Regel 3

Alle Designfaktoren und Gestaltungskriterien müssen die Möglichkeit der Übertragbarkeit von einem Medium zum andern haben und sind gleichartig anzuwenden.

Die Elemente eines Firmenerscheinungsbildes sollen wiedererkennbar in jeder Form der Firmenpräsentation sichtbar sein.

Auf der gegenüberliegenden Seite ist eine Reproduktion wiedergegeben, die ich mit freundlicher Genehmigung dem Band 1 der «Basic Design Elements and Their Systems», herausgegeben vom CoCoMAS Committee, entnommen habe.

Diese Grafik zeigt in sehr anschaulicher Weise anhand des «Mazda-Baumes», wie die einzelnen Designfaktoren übergreifend in alle Bereiche der Firmenpräsentation ein gleichartiges Erleben mit einer Firma vermitteln können:

Die Schriften sind eindeutig fixiert: Im oberen Block der Corporate Logotypes gibt es vorwiegend die Ideogramme in «kanji», also Wortbegriffen.

Im zweiten Block der Wagenschriftzüge lesen wir «katakana», eine Silbenschrifttype, die mit dem darunterstehenden lateinischen Alphabet formal zusammengeht. (Wichtig für Export!)

In (überlegtem?) Gegensatz dazu steht Opel Deutschland. Jeder Wagentyp trägt einen anderen eigenwilligen Schriftzug – nicht nur am Heck – noch einmal anders in den Anzeigen.

Die rechte Anzeige zum Beispiel hat im Textteil eine andere Manta-Schrift als auf dem Wagenschild, und über die Anzeige haben wir den Schriftzug gestellt, den wir am Kofferraum der Autos sahen.

3e règle

Tous les facteurs de design et tous les critères de conception formelle doivent être transmissibles d'un média à l'autre et applicables de manière équivalente.

Les éléments d'une image d'identification de l'entreprise doivent se retrouver, sous forme parfaitement reconnaissable, dans chaque présentation visuelle de l'entreprise.

Sur la page ci-contre figure une reproduction extraite – avec l'aimable autorisation de l'auteur – du volume I de «Basic Design Elements and Their Systems», édité par le CoCoMAS Committee.

A l'aide de l'«arbre Mazda», la représentation graphique montre de manière très éloquente comment les différents facteurs de design, appliqués à tous les secteurs de la présentation, peuvent produire une perception cohérente de l'entreprise:

Les types de caractères sont clairement fixés: le bloc supérieur des logotypes de l'entreprise comprend primairement des idéogrammes en «kanji», qui expriment l'idée du mot. Dans le deuxième bloc des inscriptions sur les véhicules, nous lisons en «katakana» des caractères d'écriture syllabique, formellement combinés à l'alphabet latin placé en dessous. (Importance pour l'exportation!)

Opel Allemagne adopte (sciemment?) la position contraire. Chaque type de voiture porte un logo bien distinct des autres, dont la conception formelle est encore une fois différente dans les annonces.

L'annonce de droite montre par exemple dans le texte une autre écriture Manta que sur la voiture même, et en haut de l'annonce a été repris le logotype placé sur le coffre à bagage.

Man muß einem besonderen Auto ja nicht unbedingt ansehen, wie vernünftig es ist. ⊖ Manta

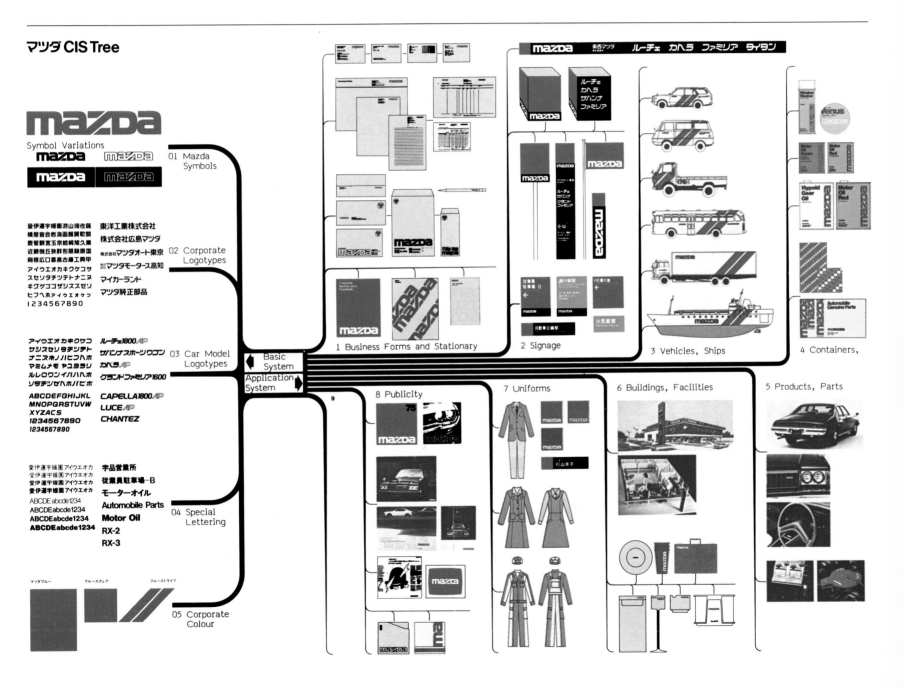

マツダ CIS Tree

MAZDA

Symbol Variations

01 Mazda Symbols

02 Corporate Logotypes

03 Car Model Logotypes

04 Special Lettering

05 Corporate Colour

Basic System

Application System

1 Business Forms and Stationary

2 Signage

3 Vehicles, Ships

4 Containers,

5 Products, Parts

6 Buildings, Facilities

7 Uniforms

8 Publicity

Rule 4

A clear identity is not the result of many individuals — and/or of manifold single activities!
Uniformity and conformity come into existence through consistency and responsible competence of one decisive (!) central authority.

Regel 4

Eine eindeutige Identity ist nicht das Ergebnis von vielen bzw. einer Vielzahl von Einzelaktivitäten!
Einheitlichkeit und Übereinstimmung entstehen nur durch Konsequenz und verantwortliche Zuständigkeit einer entscheidenden (!) Zentralstelle.

4e règle

Une Identity unique n'est pas la somme d'identités multiples, resp. d'une grande multiplicité d'activités individuelles.
La cohérence et la concordance sont le fruit d'un effort systématique et relèvent de la compétence d'une centrale déterminante (!), agissant en pleine conscience de ses responsabilités.

Federal Republic of Germany

Egypt

United Kingdom

USA

Australia

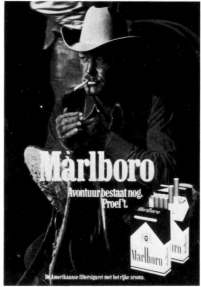

Netherlands

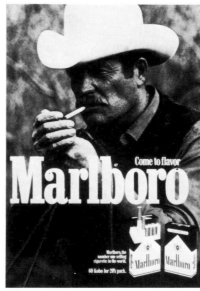

Africa

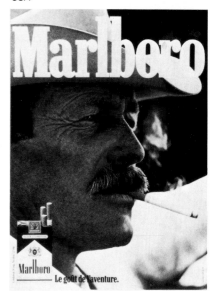

Switzerland

Rule 5

Local advertising appearances must not influence or charge the "personality" of a company.
Nationally and internationally, the design must follow the same rules of the game and at least visually have the *same positive effect,* notwithstanding the *statements* required for specific markets.

Regel 5

Die lokalen Werbeauftritte dürfen die «Persönlichkeit» des Unternehmens nicht beeinflussen oder verändern. Die Gestaltung muss national wie international den gleichen Spielregeln folgen und zumindest visuell die *gleiche Anmutung* haben, unbeschadet der marktnotwendigen *Aussagen.*

5e règle

Les présentations publicitaires locales ne doivent pas influencer ou modifier la «personnalité» de l'entreprise.
La conception formelle doit obéir aux mêmes règles de jeu, sur le plan national et international, et produire du moins la *même impression* visuelle, indépendamment de l'*expression* donnée aux messages qu'exige le marché.

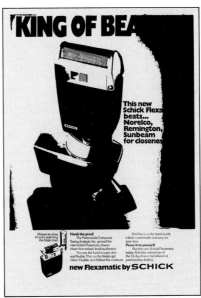

Rule 6

To possess identity means to have to create a design frame. The appearance must not change constantly. Persistence, and above all recognizability of the characteristic effect shall create confidence.

Regel 6

Identität haben heisst einen Gestaltungsrahmen schaffen. Das Erscheinungsbild darf nicht ständig wechseln. Beständigkeit und vor allem Wiedererkennbarkeit in der charakteristischen Anmutung soll Vertrauen schaffen.

6e règle

L'existence d'une identité implique la création d'un cadre pour la conception formelle. L'image d'identification ne doit pas constamment changer. Sa constance et, surtout, ses éléments de réminiscence suscitent la confiance.

Such a characteristic, classifiable picture cannot come into existence, if a known artist is used to illustrate advertisements.
All four advertisements were drawn by Tomi Ungerer. And there is no difference in style for Siegwerk Farbenfabrik, Beer, Shoes or TWA.
In "Graphic" 11/81, H. Lechner and E. Pohl say: "T. Ungerer's unmistaken style can be used for the most varying products."
The benefits for the companies, we'll see!

Ein solch charakteristisch zuordenbares Bild kann nicht entstehen, wenn ein bekannter Künstler zur Illustration der Anzeigen herangezogen wird.
Alle vier Anzeigen sind von Tomi Ungerer gezeichnet. Dabei gibt es stilistisch keinen Unterschied für Siegwerk Farbenfabrik, Bier, Schuhe oder TWA. H. Lechner und E. Pohl schreiben in «Graphik» 11/81: «T. Ungerers unverwechselbarer Stil lässt sich für die unterschiedlichsten Produkte verwenden.»
Was für die Unternehmen dabei herauskommt, sehen wir!

Une telle image spécifique à l'entreprise ne peut naître si l'on se contente de recourir à un «artiste» célèbre pour l'illustration.
Ces quatre annonces sont toutes de la main de Tomi Ungerer. Sur le plan stylistique, il n'y a pas de différence entre la fabrique de couleurs Siegwerk, la bière, les chaussures ou la TWA.
H. Lechner et E. Pohl écrivent dans «Graphik» 11/81:
«Le style typique de T. Ungerer s'applique aux produits les plus variés.»
Ce qui en résulte pour l'entreprise se passe de tout commentaire!

Rule 7

Company management must fully identify itself with its Corporate Identity, implement it in all areas and stand for it externally in every medium.

Regel 7

Die Unternehmensleitung muss sich ganz mit der Corporate Identity identifizieren, sie in allen Bereichen durchsetzen und nach aussen in jedem Medium vertreten.

7e règle

La direction de l'entreprise doit s'identifier intégralement à la CI, l'imposer dans tous les secteurs et la représenter dans chaque média.

Twelve Pensive Examples to Investigate the Seven Rules Just Established

Zwölf nachdenkliche Beispiele zur Überprüfung der vorher aufgestellten sieben Regeln

Douze exemples à méditer pour vérifier les sept règles précédemment établies

On the following twenty-four pages the value of a uniform appearance and/or the disadvantages of missing individuality and identity will be discussed.

For each individual company it appears to be primarily a question of the value that is planted into the subject of CI. Maybe some think that uniformity and CD for their brands, which is the proof for my doctrines, are rather of disadvantage to them. In this case I reckon upon their indulgent smile.

I myself am convinced of the positive effect and increase in image if there is a uniform CI.

I am certain that uniformity creates higher quality features — and that maybe for that reason my examples are exaggerated or provocative. This may be true. But if so, it was necessary for a comparative overall picture. Does not one usually leave hot irons alone and presents only the refined jewels?

This conviction and some not representative figures have, among other criteria, determined the selection of the examples.

Automobiles, for instance, are represented so frequently because this industry belongs to the group of advertisers, who spend the most money for advertising, and because, as experience shows, they have the advertisements, whose attention value is the highest.

The examples, however, must partially generalize, because I did not want to deal with *one* situation exactly — let's say Germany. Nevertheless "for obvious reasons" I had to use most of those and among them found "the most ascertaining ones", also because they were more easily understood.

Auf den folgenden vierundzwanzig Seiten sollen der Wert einer einheitlichen Anmutung bzw. die Nachteile einer mangelnden Eigenständigkeit und Profilierung beleuchtet werden. Es scheint für die einzelnen vor allem eine Frage der Wertvorstellung zu sein, die mit dem Thema CI verbunden wird. Vielleicht meinen manche in Einheitlichkeit und CD für ihre Marke, die als Beleg für meine Thesen steht, eher Nachteiliges zu sehen. Dann rechne ich auf ihr nachsichtiges Lächeln.

Ich bin von der positiven Wirkung und Imageanhebung durch eine geschlossene CI überzeugt.

Ich bin gewiss, dass sich mit Einheitlichkeit höhere Qualitätsmerkmale ergeben – dass deshalb vielleicht meine Beispiele überzeichnen oder provozieren. Kann sein. Aber dann war es zu einer vergleichenden Gesamtbetrachtung notwendig. Werden doch gemeinhin die heissen Eisen nicht angefasst und lieber die Edel-Vorzeigestücke präsentiert.

Diese Überzeugung und einige nicht repräsentative (!) Zahlen haben die Auswahl für die Beispiele mitgetragen.

Autos zum Beispiel sind deshalb so oft vertreten, weil diese Sparte zu der Gruppe Werbetreibender gehört, die mit das meiste Geld für Anzeigenwerbung ausgibt, und weil sie erfahrungsgemäss die Anzeigen mit dem höchsten Aufmerksamkeitswert hat.

Die Beispiele müssen teilweise aber pauschalisieren, weil ich nicht exakt auf *eine* Situation – sagen wir Deutschland – eingehen wollte, obwohl ich «naheliegenderweise» davon die meisten verwenden musste und wegen des besseren Verstehenkönnens die «sprechendsten» Demonstrationen finden konnte.

Les vingt-quatre pages suivantes ont pour but de révéler la valeur d'une image cohérente et les inconvénients qui résultent d'un manque de personnalité et de profil.

Il semble que pour certains le thème CI est avant tout associé à une conception définie des valeurs. Peut-être éprouvent-ils comme plutôt négatif pour leur marque – citée à l'appui de mes thèses – cette identité cohérente et le CD. Dans ce cas, je compte sur votre sourire indulgent.

Je suis persuadé qu'une CI intégrale rehausse l'effet positif et l'image de l'entreprise.

Je suis convaincu que la cohérence de l'identité permet de répondre mieux à des critères de qualité plus élevés. Sous cet aspect, mes exemples paraîtront peut-être exagérés ou provocateurs. C'est possible. Mais dans l'intérêt d'une vue générale comparative, ils sont nécessaires, d'autant plus que bien souvent les sujets délicats sont sciemment évités dans ce genre de présentation, au profit des exemples de grand prestige.

Cette conviction, ainsi que quelques chiffres non représentatifs (!), ont motivé le choix des exemples présentés.

Les automobiles sont, par exemple, si souvent représentées parce qu'il s'agit d'un secteur qui consacre le plus d'argent à la publicité-presse et que les annonces automobiles accrochent si fortement l'attention.

Les exemples montrés obligent cependant partiellement à généraliser; je ne voulais pas me confiner à *une* seule situation (typique pour l'Allemagne, p. ex.), bien que j'ai dû choisir des exemples qui me sont «proches» pour des raisons à la fois géographiques et linguistiques.

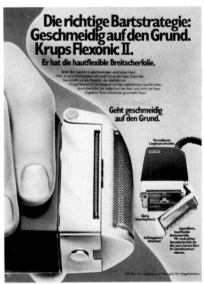

Therefore, all pictures are really representative of one thought that has moved me, and that I wanted to *illustrate* in all contrasting ways. Because my work of the past twenty years has taught me, that harmony exists only as long as concepts and visualization are only being *talked about*.

Opinions differ immediately, as soon as something can concretely be seen in the layout.

If comparative analyses were made as in this book and if one's own presentations were investigated — as I have done throughout my working life — not several angels were found with alcoholic beverages, and not several dress-up dolls from HOM and Fruit of the Loom were found, as the "Reagan dolls".
This is why Sony has probably produced its advertising handbook: "Guidelines for better advertising". From this book, let me cite the first sentence, which I like very much: "Sony never intends to follow others. Sony finds its own way to progress. Thus it has earned prestige and a high reputation."
Dankwart Rost says:
"Which entrepreneur, for instance, is not in doubt about the determination and structure of his advertising budget? …
… What success do advertisements have? What influence does the company image have on success in business? …
… What is more important: creativity or systematics? …
… Questions, which are answered by the old principle of 'trial and error' — because of a lack of generally valid knowledge."

So sind schliesslich alle Abbildungen Stellvertreter für einen bestimmten Gedanken, der mich bewegte, den ich kontrastierend *illustrieren* wollte. Weil meine Arbeit in den letzten zwanzig Jahren mich gelehrt hat, dass so lange Einigkeit herrscht, wie über Konzepte und die Visualisierung lediglich *gesprochen* wird.

Die Meinungen gehen sofort auseinander, wenn konkret etwas im Layout zu sehen ist.

Würden solche vergleichenden Zusammenstellungen wie hier und Überprüfung der eigenen Linie vorgenommen – so wie ich das während meiner ganzen Berufspraxis tat –, dann wären nicht simultan mehrere Engel bei Spirituosen zu finden und gleiche Anziehpuppen von HOM und Fruit of the Loom, wie die «Reagan-Dolls».
Wahrscheinlich hat Sony deshalb sein Handbuch für Werbung produziert: «Guidelines for better advertising». Aus diesem zitiere ich den ersten Satz, der mir sehr gut gefällt (übersetzt): «Sony beabsichtigt, nie anderen zu folgen. Sony findet seinen eigenen Weg zum Fortschritt. So sind wir zu Anerkennung und einem guten Ruf gekommen.»
Dankwart Rost sagt:
«Welcher Unternehmer ist zum Beispiel nicht im Zweifel über Bemessung und Struktur seines Werbeaufwands? …
… Welchen Erfolg bringt die Anzeigenwerbung? Wie steht es mit dem Einfluss des Firmen-Images auf den Geschäftserfolg? …
… Was ist wichtiger: Kreativität oder Systematik? …
… Fragen, die man mangels allgemeingültiger gesicherter Erkenntnisse nach dem alten Prinzip ‹trial and error› zu lösen versucht.»

Ainsi toutes les reproductions sont finalement l'expression d'une idée précise qui m'a animée et que je voulais *illustrer* par des images contrastantes.
Mon travail pendant ces 20 dernières années m'a enseigné que l'unité existe dans la mesure où l'on se contente de simplement *parler* de concepts formels et de visualisation.

Les avis divergent immédiatement dès que le layout exprime quelque chose de concret.

Des analyses comparatives (à l'instar du présent ouvrage) et la vérification critique de sa propre ligne publicitaire (comme je l'ai pratiquée pendant toute mon activité professionnelle) permettraient d'éviter l'utilisation simultanée de plusieurs anges pour différents spiritueux ou des mêmes «Reagan dolls» (poupées à habiller) chez HOM et Fruit of the Loom.
C'est probablement pour cette raison que Sony a produit son manuel sur la publicité: «Guidelines for better advertising». J'en cite la première phrase qui me plaît tout particulièrement: «Sony se propose de ne jamais suivre les autres. Sony recherche sa propre voie qui mène au succès. C'est ainsi que nous avons acquis renom et notoriété.»
Dankwart Rost dit:
«Quel est par exemple l'entrepreneur qui n'aurait des doutes sur l'envergure et la structure de ses frais publicitaires?…
… Quel résultat apporte la publicité-presse? Qu'en est-il de l'influence de l'image de marque de l'entreprise sur la rentabilité?…
… Qu'est-ce qui est plus important: la créativité ou la systématique?…
… Autant de questions que l'on essaie de résoudre selon l'ancien principe du ‹trial and error› en l'absence de connaissances générales sûres.»

① ②

③

Wo sich die Freude am Dasein in den schönsten Farben dokumentiert, ist man auch über die schönsten Formen des Genießens im Bilde: **Brandy Stock 84.**

Wir wählen die Weine für diesen Brandy aus den sechs besten Anbaugebieten Italiens. Dem Kenner erklärt sich schon daraus die Fülle und der Reichtum seines Buketts. Sorgsamste Destillation und langjährige Reifung in Eichenfässern tun ein übriges dazu. Ihnen die Wahl immer wieder zu dem Erlebnis zu machen, das Ihnen die feinen Sinne Italiens erschließt. **Brandy Stock 84.** Die feinen Sinne Italiens.

Der Anteil der Engel und "Le Paradis".

Hennessy

TIZIANO

Ein Meisterwerk in Rot von Cinzano.

„Averna schmeckt himmlisch-süß... ...und teuflisch-bitter"

AVERNA
AMARO SICILIANO – SEIN GEHEIMNIS SIND DIE KRÄUTER.

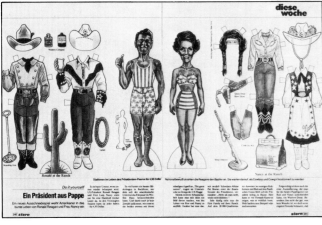

diese woche

Do it yourself
Ein Präsident aus Pappe

Ein neues Ausschneidespiel weiht Amerikaner in das bunte Leben von Ronald Reagan und Frau Nancy ein.

stern

In HOM haben Sie einen ganz neuen Auftritt

HOM

FÜR ALLE, DIE NICHT ALLES SO ENG SEHEN.

FRUIT OF THE LOOM

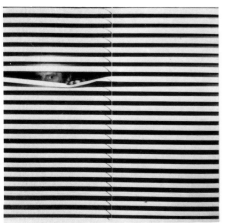

DER PREISWERTESTE WEG, UM ENDLICH AN DIE WELTBERÜHMTE OLYMPUS-BELICHTUNGSAUTOMATIK ZU KOMMEN. **OLYMPUS OM-10**

1
Front cover,
"Unorthodox Behavior"
2
Olympus advertisement,
1981

1
Schallplattenumschlag
«Unorthodox Behavior»,
2
Olympus-Anzeige, 1981

1
Couverture de disque
«Unorthodox Behavior»
2
Annonce Olympus, 1981

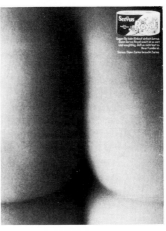

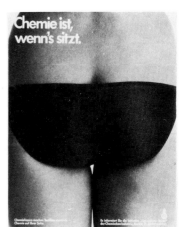

Chemie ist, wenn's sitzt.

First Example

The appearance of the company is not uniform.

The image is not rounded.

Contradictory "handwriting".

● Advertising concepts come into existence for *the one product,* without an overall plan for the future.

● Other advertisers (bottom left the Federal Postal Authority) are confusingly similar. The identity is missing.

Erstes Beispiel

Der Auftritt des Unternehmens ist uneinheitlich.

Die Anmutung nicht geschlossen. Widersprüchliche «Handschrift».

● Werbekonzepte entstehen für *das eine Produkt,* ohne Gesamtplan.

● Andere Werbetreibende (unten links die Bundespost) sind zum Verwechseln ähnlich. Eigenständigkeit fehlt.

Premier exemple

L'image de l'entreprise est incohérente. La présentation manque d'homogénéité. La «griffe» est pleine de contradictions.

● Les concepts publicitaires sont créés pour *un produit déterminé,* sans un plan global pour l'avenir.

● La publicité d'autres entreprises (en bas, à gauche, les PTT) se ressemble à s'y méprendre. Aucun trait spécifique à l'entreprise n'apparaît.

Second Example

The statements or slogans are different in different countries. Also the heterogeneous typographic treatment due to nationally imposed temperaments and preferences by Art Directors.

What is that, a slogan?
Klaus J. Moeller-Herrmann: "The personification of the company is meant to be condensed and made touchable in a slogan."
Dictionary: the catchword, the motto, the password, *the war cry.*
Mercedes obviously needs a very differentiated war cry in the individual countries.
Both with regard to "self-presentation" and with regard to the visual appearance: typefaces are arbitrarily changed, even if all over the "good star on all roads" shines.
"Slogan" has yet another translation: "fuss, pretence". For the benefit of Mercedes, I assume that even if it looks that way, pretence was not meant.
From: "Das firmenspezifische Erscheinungsbild" (The company-specific appearance), Vereinigte Glaswerke GmbH, VEGLA:
"No uniform company personality can result from individual ideas, no matter how good they are in detail …
… It is what an entrepreneur repeatedly does or how an entrepreneur reacts again and again, that lets us recognize a characteristic trait, which forms the company personality more strongly than any verbal or advertising confession …"

Exactly!

Zweites Beispiel

Die Aussagen bzw. Slogans sind in einzelnen Ländern unterschiedlich. Dazu noch heterogene typografische Behandlung durch national gefärbte Temperamente und Art-Director-Vorlieben

Was ist das, ein Slogan?
Klaus J. Moeller-Herrmann: «Die Selbstdarstellung des Unternehmens soll in einem Slogan verdichtet und griffig gemacht werden.»
Dictionary: «Das Schlagwort, der Wahlspruch, die Losung, das *Kriegsgeschrei.*»
Mercedes braucht in den einzelnen Ländern offenbar ein sehr differenziertes Kriegsgeschrei.
Sowohl was die «Selbstdarstellung» angeht als auch was den visuellen Auftritt betrifft: Schriften werden willkürlich gewechselt, selbst wenn gleichlautend der «gute Stern auf allen Strassen» leuchtet.
«Slogan» hat noch eine Übersetzung: «Das Getue.» Ich nehme zum Vorteil von Mercedes an, dass, trotz Anschein, ein Getue nicht beabsichtigt war.
Aus: «Das firmenspezifische Erscheinungsbild», Vereinigte Glaswerke GmbH, VEGLA:
«Aus einer Vielfalt von Einzelvorstellungen, und seien sie im Detail noch so gut, kann … kein einheitliches Firmenbild entstehen …
… Erst was ein Unternehmen immer wieder tut oder wie ein Unternehmer sich immer wieder verhält, erkennen wir als einen Charakterzug, der die Firmenpersönlichkeit stärker prägt als jedes Wort- oder Werbebekenntnis …»

Exakt!

Deuxième exemple

Les slogans varient d'un pays à l'autre. La conception typographique est hétérogène et change selon les tempéraments nationaux et les préférences des directeurs d'art.

Mais qu'est-ce qu'un slogan?
Klaus J. Moeller-Herrmann: «L'auto-présentation de l'entreprise doit être condensée et concrétisée en un slogan publicitaire.»
Le dictionnaire dit: «Sentence publicitaire ou de propagande, brève et frappante, appel, littéralement ‹cri de guerre›.»
Mercedes semble utiliser un «cri de guerre» très différencié, selon les pays concernés.
Tant en ce qui concerne «l'auto-présentation» (bien qu'il s'agisse de la même automobile et du même producteur), qu'en ce qui concerne la présentation visuelle: les caractères typographiques sont changés arbitrairement, même si le texte annonce toujours que la «bonne étoile brille sur toutes les routes».
Extrait de «Das firmenspezifische Erscheinungsbild» (l'image d'identification spécifique à l'entreprise), Vereinigte Glaswerke S.à r.l., VEGLA:
A partir d'une multiplicité d'idées variées – aussi bonnes soient-elles – ne peut naître une identité d'entreprise intégrée et harmonieuse...
… C'est finalement ce qu'une entreprise fait inlassablement et la manière dont elle se comporte que nous percevons comme autant de traits de caractère, qui marquent la personnalité de l'entreprise beaucoup plus qu'un acte de foi exprimé par des mots ou à coup de slogans publicitaires...»

Exact!

Mercedes-Benz
laat niets te wensen over.

Mercedes-Benz.
La sicurezza di guidare meglio.

Mercedes-Benz.
La sicurezza di guidare meglio.

Mercedes-Benz.
The sound investment.

MERCEDES-BENZ
ENGINEERED LIKE NO OTHER
CAR IN THE WORLD.

Mercedes-Benz.
Ihr guter Stern auf allen Straßen.

Mercedes-Benz
Ihr guter Stern auf allen Straßen

Mercedes-Benz
Votre bonne étoile
sur toutes les routes.

Mercedes-Benz
Votre bonne étoile sur toutes les routes.

Third Example

Even different product categories for differing target groups should recognizably show and even *benefit* from their family membership.

Drittes Beispiel

Auch verschiedene Produktkategorien für unterschiedliche Zielgruppen sollten erkennbar ihre Familienzugehörigkeit zeigen, ja vielmehr *nutzen*.

Troisième exemple

Les différentes catégories de produits, destinés à différents groupes cibles, devraient clairement exprimer leur appartenance à la même famille, voire mieux en *tirer parti*.

There are arguments against a uniform company appearance for all brands: "The manufacturer remains anonymous, remains hidden behind his brands … advantage of the 'Procter System'. Problems, sicknesses, death, which hamper one brand, but not the others. But reputation and good will just as little." (Weiland on behalf of Beiersdorf, on the right)

Even if the Procter System can still be discussed for consumer goods, for capital goods, like cars, it appears totally wrong to me. I believe Citroën is wasting goodwill because of this heterogeneous appearance. Does not this tempt one into seeing different companies behind the "pictures"? "… The purpose of Citroën's advertising is to communicate with the specified purchaser potential on an adequate level. Without taking recourse to platitudes. The style must justify both the properties of the brand, and those of the purchasers and drivers; it must coordinate both." (H. Engelmann, Gramm & Grey)

Distribution of the individual "vehicle classes" of a company over entirely different advertising agencies —with the special order to possibly win market shares from the other "class" — certainly plays the determining role for the varying appearances.

Henrion/Parkin says:
"Corporate identification works by making the design items different enough from those of other corporations not to be confused with them, and *enough like each other to carry over from one contract to another.*"

Es gibt Argumente gegen ein einheitliches Unternehmensbild für alle Marken: «Der Hersteller bleibt anonym, bleibt hinter seinen Marken versteckt … Vorteil des ‹Procter-Systems›. Probleme, Krankheit und Tod der einen Marke beeinträchtigen die anderen nicht. Aber Reputation und Goodwill ebensowenig. (Weiland für Beiersdorf, rechte Seite)

Wenn das Procter-System bei Verbrauchsgütern noch diskutierbar ist, dann scheint es mir bei Investitionsgütern, wie Autos, völlig falsch zu sein. Ich meine, Citroën vertut Goodwill mit diesem heterogenen Auftritt. Da ist man doch versucht, verschiedene Firmen hinter den «Bildern» zu sehen?
«… Aufgabe der Citroën-Werbung ist es, mit dem so beschriebenen Käuferpotential auf einer adäquaten Schiene zu kommunizieren, ohne zu Platitüden zu greifen. Der Stil muss sowohl den Eigenschaften der Marke als auch denen der Käufer und Fahrer gerecht werden, sie in Übereinstimmung bringen.» (H. Engelmann, Gramm & Grey)

Die Verteilung der einzelnen «Wagenklassen» eines Unternehmens auf ganz verschiedene Werbeagenturen – mit der Auflage, der anderen «Klasse» möglichst noch Marktanteile abzujagen – spielt für das unterschiedliche Aussehen sicher die bestimmende Rolle.

Henrion/Parkin (übersetzt):
«Ein Unternehmen findet seine Identität, indem es die einzelnen Gestaltungsaspekte von denen anderer Unternehmen unterschiedlich genug handhabt, dass sie mit jenen nicht verwechselt werden können, und einheitlich genug, dass sie von Auftritt zu Auftritt durchgängig sind.»

Il y a des arguments contre une identité intégrée de l'entreprise pour toutes les marques: «Le producteur reste anonyme, caché derrière ses marques... Avantages du ‹Procter système›. Les problèmes, les maladies et la mort d'une marque n'ont pas d'incidence sur les autres. Mais la réputation et le goodwill non plus. (Weiland pour Beiersdorf, page de droite)

Si le système Procter paraît encore discutable pour les biens de consommation, il me semble complètement erroné pour les biens d'investissement, telles les voitures.
J'estime que Citroën dilapide son goodwill avec cette présentation hétérogène.
«... Le rôle de la publicité Citroën est de communiquer par un canal adéquat avec les acheteurs, sans tomber dans les platitudes. Le style doit répondre à la fois aux qualités de la marque et aux expectations des acheteurs et conducteurs, en établissant une concordance entre les deux.» (H. Engelmann, Gramm & Grey)

L'attribution de la publicité pour les diverses «catégories de voitures» d'une même entreprise à des agences de publicité différentes, joue certainement un rôle prépondérant dans la présentation peu harmonieuse de l'entreprise.

Henrion/Parkin écrivent:
«Une entreprise trouve son identité en conférant à sa conception visuelle des aspects suffisamment distincts des autres entreprises pour que toute confusion soit exclue, et *suffisamment intégrés pour donner de l'entreprise une image harmonisée d'une présentation à l'autre*.»

Fourth Example

Contrary to the "dissolution" of a Corporate Design on the left-hand side, here is the attempt of unification due to a uniform Corporate Design element.

Viertes Beispiel

Gegen die «Auflösung» eines Corporate Design (links) ist hier der Versuch einer Zusammenbindung durch ein einheitliches Corporate-Design-Element vorgestellt.

Quatrième exemple

La «dissolution» d'un Corporate Design (à gauche) peut être palliée par une tentative de cohésion, avec un élément CD homogène.

"The CI element in its design and position is a binding first and leading step towards the creation of an advertisement; it is an integral part of the advertisement" (again Weiland when introducing the Corporate Symbol BDF).

What I mean is: The four points, which can be found at the bottom of *each* advertisement, do *not* create an *identity* in the sense of a mutually supporting and reinforced corporate appearances (the more so, as we found more companies with similar points, see on the right).

The lack of a common *attitude* is not only visible from the advertisement topics, but it also shows in the manifold packagings. A recognizable coherent overall image is missing. In my opinion, however, it would contribute towards preferring a BDF product rather than a competitive product, because one was satisfied with another one from BDF.

«Das CI-Element in seiner Gestaltung und Stellung ist eine verbindliche Vorgabe für die Gestaltung einer Anzeige, ist Bestandteil der Anzeige» (noch einmal Weiland bei Einführung des Firmensymbols (BDF).
Ich meine: Die vier Punkte, die am Fuss *jeder* Anzeige stehen, schaffen *keine Identity* im Sinne eines sich gegenseitig unterstützenden und stärkenden Firmenauftritts. (Zumal wir noch mehr Unternehmen mit ähnlichen Punkten fanden, siehe rechts.)
Das Fehlen einer gemeinsamen *Haltung* zeigt sich auch in der Vielgestaltigkeit der Packungsanmutungen. Ein wiedererkennbares zusammenhängendes Gesamtbild fehlt. Das würde aber meines Erachtens dazu beitragen, dass ein Produkt aus der BDF-Palette einem Konkurrenzprodukt vorgezogen wird, weil man mit einem anderen von BDF schon gute Erfahrung gemacht hat.

«Par sa conception et son rôle, l'élément CI constitue une caractéristique contraignante pour la création d'une annonce et devient partie intégrante de cette annonce.» (Weiland: introduction du «symbole d'entreprise BDF»).
Je pense que les quatre points qui figurent au bas de *chaque* annonce ne créent *pas d'identité.* (D'autant plus qu'il existe encore d'autres entreprises utilisant des points semblables.)
L'absence d'une *attitude* commune ressort aussi de la grande diversité de présentation des conditionnements. L'image globale et harmonisée, facile à reconnaître, manque. Or, elle pourrait contribuer à assurer à un produit de la gamme BDF la préférence par rapport à un produit de la concurrence, en raison des bonnes expériences déjà faites antérieurement par le consommateur avec un produit BDF.

Dreipunkt
Polstermöbelfabrik
artCollection
Postfach 80, 7322 D

Hamburger Werkstatt
für Behinderte GmbH

Fifth Example

"Advertising Personality" does not replace Corporate Identity, no matter how good and coherent an advertising campaign is.

Fünftes Beispiel

«Advertising Personality» ersetzt nicht die Unternehmensidentity, selbst wenn eine Werbekampagne noch so gut und in sich übereinstimmend ist.

Cinquième exemple

L'«Advertising personality» ne remplace pas l'identité d'une entreprise, même pas lorsqu'une campagne publicitaire est excellente et parfaitement cohérente.

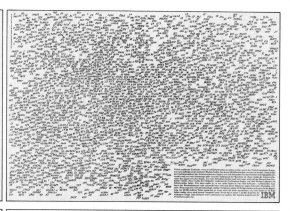

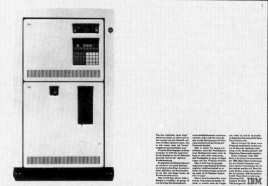

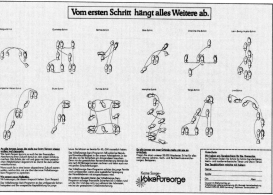

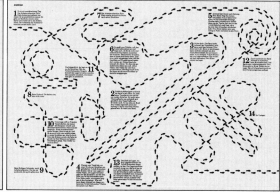

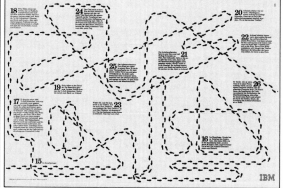

Even similarities with advertisements of other companies (who have trodden along the same path) are unavoidable. After all, others too think in terms of campaings, and not of the company image.

Sogar Ähnlichkeiten mit Anzeigen anderer Firmen (mit gleich drolligen Fussstapfen) sind unvermeidlich. Schliesslich denken auch andere in Kampagnen und nicht ans Firmenbild.

Les similitudes avec des annonces d'autres sociétés (mêmes traces de pas amusantes) sont inévitables. Car les autres entreprises ont aussi oublié leur image d'entreprise.

32

Spectacular advertising appearances counteract identity and efface the personality of a company. "Funny" advertisements are above all made for the jurors of the Art Directors Club!

Spektakuläre Werbeauftritte wirken einer Identity entgegen, verwischen die Eigenheit des Unternehmens. «Witzige» Anzeigen werden doch zuerst einmal für die Juroren vom Art Directos Club gemacht!

Les présentations publicitaires spectaculaires sont contraires à la Corporate Identity, estompent les traits caractéristiques de l'entreprise. Quant aux annonces «pleines d'esprit», elles sont d'abord faites pour le jury du Art Directors Club!

In this labyrinth of varying layouts (and qualities!) the chameleon-like changing of a corporation becomes visible, rather than a mutual spirit of all concerned.

In diesem Labyrinth unterschiedlicher Layouts (und Qualitäten!) ist eher die chamäleonhafte Wandlung eines Konzerns auszumachen als ein allen gemeinsamer Geist.

A travers le dédale des layouts (et des qualités) si variés, ce sont les perpétuels changements qui s'expriment plutôt que l'esprit commun à toute la société.

Non-endingly repeated rhymes are subject to wear. They get to be propaganda slogans (with all of their unpleasant after-taste). They do not create a company personality.

Penetrant wiederholte Sprüche nützen sich schnell ab. Sie werden zu Propagandaparolen (mit allem unangenehmen Beigeschmack). Eine Unternehmenspersönlichkeit schaffen sie nicht.

Les slogans répétés jusqu'à outrance s'usent rapidement. Ils deviennent des paroles propagandistes (avec toute la connotation négative de ce terme). Ils ne concourent pas à la personnalité de l'entreprise.

Our name is enough.

Olympus already says it in a totally over-exaggerated way. And also Rothmans, "One of the world's greatest names".

Just as the examples on the right are representative for the narcism of this kind of boasting.

Olympus sagt es in seiner Überzogenheit schon. Auch Rothmans, «One of the world's greatest names».

So, wie die Beispiele rechts stellvertretend für die narzisstische Manie dieser Art des Sprüchemachens stehen.

«Olympus», Olympe, est un exemple typique de ce genre. De même que Rothmans, «one of the world's greatest names».

Tout comme les exemples à droite sont l'expression de cette manie narcissiste de fabriquer des aphorismes.

OLYMPUS
Our name is enough.

OLYMPUS
Unser Name genügt.

OLYMPUS
Notre nom suffit.

VW
More than a car.

VW
Mehr als Autos.

VW
Plus que des autos.

CITROËN
Intelligence on wheels.

CITROËN
Intelligenz auf Rädern.

CITROËN
L'intelligence sur roues.

MIELE
There is nothing better.

MIELE
Da ist keine bessere.

MIELE
Il n'en est pas de meilleure.

LONGINES
The style of the present

LONGINES
Der Stil der Zeit

LONGINES
Le style du temps

GRUNDIG
The safety of a great name

GRUNDIG
Die Sicherheit eines grossen Namens

GRUNDIG
La sécurité d'un grand nom

One thing is safe.
BOSCH

Eins ist sicher.
BOSCH

Une chose est sûre.
BOSCH

Z is for ZANUSSI

Z steht für ZANUSSI

Z pour ZANUSSI

LURGI

Just as worn off as slogans (or even more) is the globe, and therefore entirely unsuitable for an identity. Only the "view" of the globe (depending on the location) varies.

Abgewetzt wie Sprüche (oder mehr) ist die Weltkugel. Deshalb als Träger für eine Identity völlig ungeeignet. Nur die «Sicht» auf die Kugel (je nach Standort) variiert.

L'image du globe terrestre est usée à l'excès, à l'instar de certains slogans, peut-être même plus. Elle est donc inappropriée comme support pour une identité d'entreprise. Seule la «vue» sur le globe varie (selon le lieu d'implantation de l'entreprise).

SPERRY **Mit uns kann man reden.**

océ *Wir wissen, wie wichtig Zuhören ist.*

3M WIR ANTWORTEN.

Sperry: We can be talked to
océ: We know how important it is to listen.
3M: We answer.

Sperry: Avec nous on peut parler
océ: Nous savons combien il est
important d'être à l'écoute.
3M: Nous répondons.

If you read the three "slogans" above from Sperry, océ and 3M one after the other, a funny sequence of sentences develops. Similar to the opposite page.
This page exclusively presents innovators:

Liest man die drei «Sprüche» oben von Sperry, océ und 3M hintereinander, wird eine komische Satzreihe daraus. Ähnlich wie bei der gegenüberliegenden Seite.
Auf dieser Seite stellen sich ausschliesslich Erfinder vor.

Si on lit l'un après l'autre les trois slogans de Sperry, océ et 3M cités plus haut, une séquence de phrases inattendue en résulte. Tout comme pour la page ci-contre.
Sur cette page, des inventeurs se présentent.

Fichtel & Sachs The innovator AG	Fichtel & Sachs Die Erfinder AG	Fichtel & Sachs SA des inventions	**Fichtel & Sachs.** **Die Erfinder AG.** SACHS
Fun in Innovating TOSHIBA	Spass am Erfinden TOSHIBA	Le plaisir d'inventer TOSHIBA	**Spass** **am Erfinden** **TOSHIBA**
Fifty Years of Innovation TEXAS INSTRUMENTS	Fünfzig Jahre der Erfindung. TEXAS INSTRUMENTS	Cinquante années d'innovations TEXAS INSTRUMENTS	Fifty Years of Innovation TEXAS INSTRUMENTS
TELEFUNKEN Experienced in Innovation	TELEFUNKEN Erfahren im Erfinden.	TELEFUNKEN Expérimenté dans l'invention.	**TELEFUNKEN** **Erfahren im Erfinden.**
GILLETTE From Gillette, the people who have innovated shaving with the razor blade	GILLETTE Von Gillette, den Leuten, die das Rasieren mit der Klinge erfunden haben	GILETTE De Gilette, à ceux qui ont inventé le rasage à la lame.	Gillette *Von Gillette, den Leuten, die das Rasieren mit der Klinge erfunden haben.*
JVC The Innovator of the VHS System	JVC Der Erfinder des VHS-Systems	JVC L'inventeur du système VHS	**JVC** **Der Erfinder des VHS-Systems**
RADO Innovator of the scratch-resistant watch	RADO Der Erfinder der kratzfesten Uhr.	RADO Inventeur de la montre inrayable.	**RADO** Erfinder der kratzfesten Uhr.
from the Innovator of Video Cassettes SONY	vom Erfinder der Video-Cassetten. SONY	de l'inventeur des cassettes vidéo. SONY	**vom** **Erfinder der Video-Cassetten.** **SONY.**

FREEDOM NEEDS FREE ENTERPRISE

Experience, expertise and teamwork - worldwide

Original signs, typeface and slogans of an American advertisement

Originalzeichen, Schrift und Slogan aus einer amerikanischen Anzeige.

Symbole original, caractères et slogan d'une annonce américaine.

COLONIA Trust us—and your brains.	COLONIA Vertrauen Sie uns – und Ihrem Verstand	COLONIA Faites-nous confiance – ainsi qu'à votre raison.	**COLONIA** **Vertrauen Sie uns –** **und Ihrem Verstand.**
TOYOTA Trust your brains	TOYOTA Vertrauen Sie Ihrem Verstand	TOYOTA Faites confiance à votre raison.	**TOYOTA** Vertrauen Sie Ihrem Verstand
SAAB Strength and Brains.	SAAB Kraft und Verstand	SAAB Force et raison.	**SAAB** Kraft und Verstand.
FORD The symbol of reason.	FORD Das Zeichen der Vernunft	FORD Le signe du bon sens.	**Ford** Das Zeichen der Vernunft.
VW The Scirocco Excitingly reasonable.	VW Der Scirocco. Aufregend vernünftig.	VW La Scirocco. Raisonnable jusqu'à l'émoi.	**Der Scirocco.** **Aufregend vernünftig.**
FIAT Very close to the ideal	FIAT Ganz nahe am Ideal	FIAT Proche de l'idéal.	**FIAT** Ganz nahe am Ideal
BANG & OLUFSON We think differently.	BANG & OLUFSEN Wir denken anders.	BANG & OLUFSEN Nous pensons différemment.	**Bang & Olufsen** We think differently.
RENA The better solution comes from us.	RENA Die bessere Lösung kommt von uns.	RENA La meilleure solution vient de chez nous.	**RENA** *Die bessere Lösung kommt von uns.*
TEXACO Trust Texaco to think ahead.	TEXACO Vertrauen Sie Texaco, weiter zu denken	TEXACO Faites confiance à Texaco pour penser plus loin.	**TEXACO** TRUST TEXACO TO THINK AHEAD.
Think further! SHELL	Weiter denken! SHELL	Penser plus loin! SHELL	**Weiter denken!** Shell

Seventh Example

Logotypes are only a small portion of an identity. Originally, the boss and his signature stood for the company. These two elements carried the company's personality to the outside representatively. This was something like the company symbol, without a firm intention towards design.

From the design guidelines by Merck: *"Forms of application of the company sign and the logotype":*
"Company sign of E. Merck, Darmstadt, is the trademark Merck in capital letters …
The logotype E. Merck must only be used, when it serves as a declaration of warranty in the form of a signature …"

From a presentation of Paul Rand in 1966 concerning modernization of the old Ford brand.
"The graphics of 1900 were in a sense a product of the time: life was more elaborate, more ceremonious … Industrial graphics, like 'Home, Sweet Home', were a kind of sentimental sedative, a style which, even today, would be eminently more suited to a make-belief world, to the circus and amusement park, to pink lemonade and soda pop, than to the practical world of the machine.
Makers not only of automobiles, but of coffee machines and lawn mowers, face powders, drugsand corn plasters signed their wares in this anonymous style. The world was flooded with 'heavied up' scripts, fancy frills and shapely frames. Ironically, what started out to be less a mark of its maker than of its time …"

Siebtes Beispiel

Schriftzüge sind nur ein kleiner Teil einer Identity. Ursprünglich stand der Chef und seine Unterschrift für die Firma. Sie trugen die Unternehmenspersönlichkeit stellvertretend nach draussen. Daraus wurden so etwas wie Firmenzeichen ohne festen Gestaltungswillen.

Aus den Gestaltungsrichtlinien von Merck: «*Andwendungsformen des Firmenzeichens und des Namenszuges*»:
«Firmenzeichen der E. Merck, Darmstadt, ist die Wort-Marke Merck in Versalien …
… Der Namenszug E. Merck soll nur zur Anwendung kommen, wo er als eine unterschriftliche Garantieerklärung angebracht ist …»

Aus einer Präsentation von Paul Rand, 1966, die alte Ford-Marke zu modernisieren (übersetzt):
«Die Grafiken von 1900 waren in gewissem Sinn ein Produkt der Zeit: Das Leben war umständlicher, feierlicher … Industriegrafiken, wie ‹Home, sweet home› waren eine Art gefühlvolles Beruhigungsmittel, ein Stil, der selbst heute viel, viel besser in eine Traumwelt, in den Zirkus und Unterhaltungspark, zu rosa und anderen Limonaden passte als in die praktische Welt der Maschine. Nicht nur die Hersteller von Autos, sondern auch von Kaffeemaschinen und Rasenmähern, von Pudern und Hühneraugenpflastern unterzeichneten ihre Produkte auf diese anonyme Art. Die Welt war von ‹beschwerten› Schriften, Schnörkeln und ausgefallenen Rahmen überflutet. Paradoxerweise wurde das, was ursprünglich die Unterschrift eines einzelnen und seines Produktes sein sollte, nicht zum Symbol des Produzenten, sondern dem seiner Zeit …»

Septième exemple

Les logotypes ne constituent qu'une petite partie d'une identité. A l'origine, le chef de l'entreprise se portait garant de la société, moyennant l'apposition de sa signature. Plus tard, ce rôle incombait au symbole d'entreprise, souvent réalisé sans souci de création formelle.

Extrait des directives de Merck sur la conception graphique: «*Formes d'application du symbole et du logotype de l'entreprise*»:
«Le symbole de l'entreprise E. Merck, Darmstadt, est la marque verbale Merck en capitales…
… Le logotype E. Merck ne trouve application que là où une déclaration de garantie écrite, sous forme de signature, paraît indiquée…»

Extrait d'une présentation de Paul Rand en 1966 pour moderniser l'ancienne marque Ford:
«Les graphismes de 1900 étaient dans un certain sens un produit de leur temps: la vie était plus compliquée, plus sophistiquée… Les graphismes industriels, tels que ‹Home, sweet home›, constituaient une sorte de soporifique sentimental, un style qui – aujourd'hui encore – convient bien mieux au monde du rêve, du cirque et du divertissement, qui correspondait mieux aux limonades roses et autres boissons édulcorées qu'au monde pratique de la machine. Nous seulement les fabricants d'automobiles, mais aussi les producteurs de machines à café et de tondeuses à gazon, de poudres et de remèdes contre les cors aux pieds parafaient leurs produits de cette manière anonyme. Le monde était submergé de caractères ‹alourdis d'empattements›, d'ornements et de fioritures diverses. Paradoxalement, ce qui à l'origine devait être la griffe d'une personne ou d'un produit, n'est pas devenu le symbole du producteur, mais celui de son époque…»

I made an experiment. The two symbols of "Ford" and "Esso" were just about exchanged:
1. The name remained, but the oval of the two was exchanged.
2. The oval is correct, but the italics of "Ford" were removed, and "Esso" was italizised.
In my opinion it is of less significance that I reversed the blue/negative Ford — but, to be correct, it should be mentioned.
28 people (creatives, contacters and advertising agency experts) were confronted with this falsified symbol. Among them were seven persons who actively handled the Ford account. Only 10 noticed the exchange.
This game should only point out one phenomenon, which is known about witnessing statements: our memory is ususally rather incomplete when it comes to details. Just make the well-known experiment: cover up your wrist watch without looking at it. What kind of numbers does it have? Roman, Arabic, points, lines?

"… from memory only 10% of the test persons could sketch the Aral symbol correctly …"
(R. Mielke in "Corporate Identity")
Having made this experiment, by no means do I want to abolish the brand-mark, logos or symbols. I am convinced that they are necessary — especially the consistent application of Ford and Esso proves this. Only the absolute belief in the brand should be scattered:
If the overall picture does not also signal Ford, in spite of the signature no clear identification can be reached.

Ich habe ein Experiment veranlasst: Die beiden Zeichen «Ford» und «Esso» wurden gewissermassen vertauscht.
1. Der Namenszug blieb, aber das Oval der beiden ist ausgewechselt.
2. Das Oval ist korrekt, aber die Kursivlage bei «Ford» aufgehoben, dafür wurde «Esso» kursiv gestellt.
Dass ich dabei das sonst blau-negative Ford-Zeichen positiv umkehrte, hat meines Erachtens untergeordnete Bedeutung – sei aber der Korrektheit wegen erwähnt.
28 Personen (Kreativen, Kontaktern und Sachbearbeitern einer Werbeagentur) wurden diese verfälschten Zeichen vorgelegt. Darunter waren 7, die selbst am Ford-Etat arbeiten. Nur 10 Personen haben das Wechselspiel durchschaut.
Ich will mit diesem Spiel nur auf ein Phänomen hinweisen, das von Zeugenaussagen bekannt ist: Wir haben zumeist ein sehr lückenhaftes Gedächtnis, wenn es um Details geht. Machen Sie den bekannten Versuch: Decken Sie Ihre Armbanduhr ab, ohne draufzuschauen. Welche Art Zahlen hat sie? Römische, arabische, Punkte, Striche?

«… lediglich 10% der Befragten konnten aus der Erinnerung das Aral-Zeichen richtig skizzieren …» (R. Mielke in «Corporate Identity»)
Keineswegs möchte ich mit diesem Exkurs die Markenzeichen, Logos oder Symbole abschaffen. Ich glaube, dass sie notwendig sind – gerade die konsequente Anwendung von Ford und Esso belegt das. Nur die absolute Markengläubigkeit soll erschüttert werden:
Wenn das Gesamtbild nicht ebenfalls Ford signalisiert, kommt es trotz Unterschrift zu keiner eindeutigen Identifizierung.

Je me suis livré à une expérience dans laquelle les deux signes «Ford» et «Esso» ont été en quelque sorte interchangés.
1. Le logotype reste, mais l'ovale des deux signes est permuté.
2. L'ovale est correct, mais la position légèrement inclinée des caractères chez «Ford» a été redressée, par contre, l'écriture «Esso» est mise en italique.
Le fait d'avoir transformé le signe bleu-négatif Ford en un signe positif n'a qu'une importance secondaire.
Les symboles ainsi «truqués» ont été soumis à 28 personnes, toutes d'une agence de publicité (créateurs, responsables des contacts et spécialistes publicitaires). 10 personnes seulement ont décelé le subterfuge.
Par ce petit jeu, je voulais simplement attirer l'attention sur un phénomène bien connu dans les dépositions des témoins: notre mémoire est en général très défaillante lorsqu'il s'agit des menus détails. Livrez-vous, pour vous en convaincre, à l'essai bien connu que voici: Recouvrez votre montre-bracelet, sans l'avoir d'abord regardée. Quel genre de chiffres a-t-elle? Des chiffres romains, arabes, des points, des traits?

«… 10% à peine des personnes interrogées ont pu dessiner correctement de mémoire le symbole Aral…»
(R. Mielke dans «Corporate Identity»)
Cette digression du sujet n'a aucunement pour but de proposer la suppression des symboles, signes distinctifs ou logotypes de marques. Il s'agit simplement d'ébranler la foi aveugle et absolue dans la marque.
Si l'image globale ne signale pas qu'il s'agit de Ford, aucune identification claire et sans équivoque n'est possible, malgré la griffe apposée.

Père Magloire, Calvados

Eighth Example

Company-signs do not make a corporate personality either, even if some companies have "personalized" signs. "Some advertising agencies are doing that by trying to describe the product as a person. Jell-O, for example, is that very nice lady who lives next door." (J. Plummer)
Roman Antonoff: "A Chairman of the Board is not the corporation itself, but his face can be the company face … *but by no means the signet.*"
This shows that one also speaks of the "company face". Certainly, at the beginning of the development of company symbols or the "label" of a certain product, the head or figure has had the function of giving the brand a personality:

Achtes Beispiel

Firmenzeichen machen keine Unternehmenspersönlichkeit. Wenn auch manche Unternehmen «figürliche» Zeichen haben.
«Einige Werbeagenturen … versuchen, das Produkt als Person zu beschreiben. Jell-O zum Beispiel ist die sehr liebe Dame, die nebenan wohnt.» (J. Plummer)
Roman Antonoff: «Ein Vorstandsvorsitzender ist zwar nicht die Firma selbst, doch sein Gesicht kann das Firmengesicht sein … *und nicht etwa das Signet.*»
Man spricht also auch vom «Firmengesicht». Sicher hatte zu Beginn der Firmenzeichenentwicklung oder des «Etiketts» für ein bestimmtes Produkt der Kopf oder die Figur die Funktion, der Marke eine Persönlichkeit zu geben:

Huitième exemple

Les signes d'entreprise ne font pas encore la personnalité d'une société, même si certaines entreprises se servent de signes figuratifs.
«Certaines agences de publicité… essayent de décrire le produit à la manière d'une personne. Jell-O, par exemple, est la très gentille dame qui habite juste à côté.» (J. Plummer)
Roman Antonoff: «Le président du Conseil d'administration *n'est pas* l'entreprise en tant que telle, mais son visage peut être celui de l'entreprise…»
On parle donc bien du «visage» de l'entreprise. Au début du développement du symbole d'une entreprise ou de l'«étiquette» d'un produit déterminé, la tête ou la silhouette avait pour fonction de conférer une personnalité à la marque:

WILLIAMS & HUMBERT

THE DON

Certain "characters" were invented to personalize a brand and to give it quality: in the course of time these "persons" were more and more abstracted, like the composed Napoleon or the Oetker lady. The intention was to give the product human closeness or "warmth". Subsequently, the designers abstracted more and more.
Along with the continuing "brand symbol flooding" — along with the permanent design fever — more and more impersonal, totally abstract "figures" emerged: a ring (the symbol!) for a British cement factory and interchangeably, the emblem of the German opticians (on the right, one above the other).

Bestimmte «Typen» wurden erfunden, um der Marke Charakter und auch ein Gütesiegel mitzugeben: Der stilisierte Napoleon oder die Oetkers-Frau. Die Absicht war dabei, dem Produkt sogenannte menschliche Nähe oder «Wärme» mitzugeben. Dann haben die Designer immer weiter abstrahiert:
So kamen mit der fortschreitenden «Markenzeichen-Schwemme» – der permanenten Gestaltungslust – immer unpersönlichere, ganz und gar abstrakte «Figuren»: Ein Ring (das Symbol!) für eine britische Zementfabrik und, austauschbar, das Emblem der deutschen Augenoptiker (rechts untereinander).

Certains «personnages» ont été inventés pour donner du caractère à la marque et pour la doter d'un label de qualité: pensons au personnage stylisé de Napoléon ou à la femme d'Oetker. L'intention est de conférer au produit une sorte de «chaleur» humaine. Puis les «concepteurs» ont créé des personnages toujours plus abstraits. La vogue croissante des symboles de marque et la propension à la création graphique ont fini par produire des «figures» toujours plus impersonnelles et de plus en plus abstraites: un anneau est le symbole d'une cimenterie britannique et (signe interchangeable!) l'emblème des opticiens allemands. (A droite, l'un sous l'autre.)

BLUE CIRCLE

Leistungsgemeinschaft
Deutscher Augenoptiker.

Discursive thoughts and quotations on the design of symbols and on the value of abstraction in particular.

Underneath are three pictograms or signs: Karl Radlbeck, who, in these flashes of wit, makes fun of the blown-up passion for drawing.

Abschweifende Gedanken und Zitate über Zeichengestaltung und über den Wert der Abstraktion im besonderen.

Darunter stehen drei Piktogramme oder Bildzeichen: Karl Radlbeck, der mit diesen spassigen Einfällen die Aufgeblähtheit der Zeichensucht auf den Arm nimmt.

Digressions et citations sur la conception formelle des signes et, en particulier, sur la valeur de l'abstraction.

Trois «pictogrammes» ou images de symboles: Karl Radlbeck qui, par ces dessins humoristiques, ridiculise l'engouement prétentieux pour les symboles.

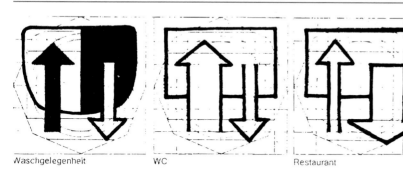
Waschgelegenheit   WC   Restaurant

Washroom
Toilet
Restaurant

Waschgelegenheit
Toilette (WC)
Restaurant

Toilettes
WC
Restaurant

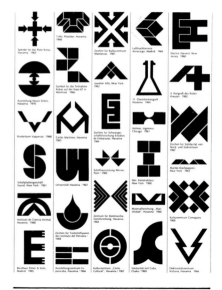

H. Heiderhoff relating to the shown drafts by Felix Beltram (Cuba):
'Advertising that decides in favour of using symbolic, logical symbols, just about counts upon an intelligent consumer. From that understanding, such advertising points to the future …
… In that way, intelligent advertising remains faithful to the more familiar handling of symbols in a wider sense, and symbolic signs (pictures) in the conventional understanding of the narrower meaning."

This is mere nonsense! It was nevertheless quoted so broadly, because it appears to me symptomatic for the thinking and working style of quite a few CD "design factories". I myself go along with David Ogilvy (quoted from a German translation):
"Trademarks and symbols were very valuable in older times, because this way even illiterates could recognize their advertisements. But illiteracy has now disappeared in the United States, and *you can rely on the fact that the printed word is understood."*

Maybe at Alcantara someone has read Ogilvy and therefore added to the signet that "Alcantara is the symbol for the brand". What else?
But it is altogether certain that it was necessary for Zeiss to explain what the symbol means.

H. Heiderhoff zu nebenstehenden Zeichenentwürfen von F. Beltram (Kuba):
«Eine Werbung, die sich zur Einsetzung symbolischer Logikzeichen entschliesst, rechnet geradezu mit einem intelligenten Konsumenten. In diesem Sinne ist solche Werbung zukunftweisend …
… So bleibt intelligente Werbung bisweilen noch dem vertrauteren Umgang mit Symbolen im weiteren und Symbolzeichen (-bildern) in der herkömmlichen Fassung des engeren Sinnes treu.»

Das ist blanker Unsinn! Es ist trotzdem so breit zitiert, weil es mir symptomatisch scheint für Denken und Arbeitsstil mancher CD-«Designfabrik». Ich halte es mit David Ogilvy: «Markenzeichen und Symbole waren in früherer Zeit sehr wertvoll, denn so konnten selbst Analphabeten ihre Anzeige erkennen. Aber das Analphabetentum ist in den Vereinigten Staaten nunmehr verschwunden, und *Sie können sich ruhig darauf verlassen, dass man gedruckte Wörter versteht.»*

Vielleicht hat man bei Alcantara Ogilvy gelesen und deshalb noch zum Signet geschrieben, dass «Alcantara das Zeichen für die Marke» sei. Was sonst? Ganz sicher aber war es für Zeiss nötig, zu erklären, was das Symbol soll.

H. Heiderhoff commente ainsi les croquis ci-contre de Felix Beltram (Cuba): «Une publicité qui décide de se servir de signes logiques comme symboles mise littéralement sur un consommateur intelligent.
… C'est ainsi que la publicité intelligente reste parfois fidèle à l'usage familier des symboles, au sens large du terme, et des signes (ou images) symboliques, au sens traditionnel plus restreint.»

Voilà bien un parfait non-sens! Cette déclaration me semble symptomatique pour le mode de pensée et de travail de mainte «fabrique de design» produisant des CD. Je préfère me rallier à l'avis de David Ogilvy:
«Les signes distinctifs de marque et les symboles étaient jadis fort précieux, car ainsi même les analphabets pouvaient reconnaître leur annonce. Mais l'analphabétisme a désormais disparu aux Etats-Unis et *vous pouvez être rassurés: les mots imprimés seront compris.»*

Peut-être a-t-on lu Ogilvy, chez «Alcantara», ce qui expliquerait pourquoi l'emblème a été complété par la phrase «Alcantara est le signe distinctif de la marque».
Sans aucun doute, Zeiss a estimé nécessaire d'expliquer son symbole.

DAS ZEICHEN FÜR DIE MARKE

 Symbol für Zeiss Qualität.

CONSOLIDATED FOODS CORPORATION

klöber
Die Freiheit,
besser zu sitzen.

Ninth Example

In particular the very much abstracted inconcrete signs or logos are questionable as carriers of an intended identity.
In Germany today there are more than 227,000 registered trademarks, while the records of the German Patent Office in Munich include nearly a million, including those that have lapsed. From these abstract formations a personality can only be created for a long period of time and characterized by continuous repetition at a high expense. This becomes particularly evident, if we look at the (influenced or accidental) similarities and duplications on these pages. There is hardly any possibility left to develop original, clever and non-interchangeable "pictures". Considering the designers' compulsion to draw and the logo inflation, mix-ups are unavoidable for the onlooker.
I do not speak of plagiarism! I just want to ascertain that a designer today has hardly any possibility of creating something "different", something unique, and thus give a company an individual position at least in this field.
All companies starting their identity with a sign should keep this in mind. Self-comprehension, overall style and individuality are the prerequisites for a convincing appearance!
"… Companies having a clearly defined appearance enter consciousness even before the desire or necessity crops up to occupy oneself with their product." (VEGLA)

Neuntes Beispiel

Grade die stark abstrahierten, nicht konkreten Zeichen oder Logos sind als Träger einer beabsichtigten Identity fragwürdig.
«In Deutschland gibt es heute mehr als 227 000 eingetragene Warenzeichen. Beim Deutschen Patentamt in München liegen fast eine Million vor, einschliesslich jener, die abgelaufen sind.»
Eine Personality kann aus diesen abstrakten Gebilden nur mit grossem geldlichen Aufwand, über lange Zeit und mit konstanter Wiederholung aufgebaut werden. Besonders deutlich wird das, wenn wir uns die (beeinflussten oder zufälligen) Ähnlichkeiten und Duplikate auf diesen Seiten ansehen. Es gibt kaum noch die Möglichkeit, originäre, gescheite und unverwechselbare «Gestalten» zu entwickeln. Verwechslungen sind für den Aussenstehenden bei der Zeichenwut der Gestalter und der Logotype-Inflation unvermeidlich.
Ich spreche nicht von Plagiaten! Ich möchte nur feststellen, dass es einem Grafiker heutzutage kaum noch möglich sein dürfte, etwas «anderes», Einmaliges zu erfinden und damit dem Unternehmen wenigstens in diesem Bereich Alleinstellung zu geben.
Das sollten sich alle Unternehmen vor Augen halten, die ihre Identity mit einem Zeichen beginnen. Selbstverständnis, Gesamtstil und Eigenart sind die Voraussetzung für einen überzeugenden Auftritt!
«… Unternehmen mit einem festen Erscheinungsbild treten bereits ins Bewusstsein, bevor der Wunsch oder die Notwendigkeit auftritt, sich mit ihren Produkten zu beschäftigen.» (VEGLA)

Neuvième exemple

Les signes ou logos abstraits sont des moyens très imparfaits pour exprimer l'identité d'une entreprise. Plus de 227 000 marques sont actuellement déposées en Allemagne. Le Bureau allemand des brevets à Munich en a enregistré près d'un million, y compris les marques périmées.
A partir de telles configurations abstraites, il n'est possible de forger une «personnalité» d'entreprise qu'au prix de gros investissements de temps et d'argent et de constantes répétitions. Cette constatation devient encore plus évidente à la lumière des nombreuses similitudes (voulues ou aléatoires) et des doublets présentés sur ces pages. Les possibilités de développer encore des formes originales, pertinentes et uniques sont minimes. Pour le «non-initié», les confusions sont inévitables face à l'acharnement créatif de certains designers et à l'inflation généralisée des logotypes.
Je ne parle pas de plagiat! Je tiens simplement à constater qu'il est difficilement possible à un graphiste de nos jours d'inventer quelque chose de «différent», d'unique, pour conférer ainsi à l'entreprise une position inégalée, du moins dans ce domaine.
Toute entreprise qui commence son «Identity» par un symbole devrait bien se pénétrer de cette idée.
La perception claire de ses valeurs inhérentes, le style global et l'originalité de l'entreprise, telles sont les prémisses de toute présentation convaincante!
«… Les entreprises disposant d'une forte image d'identification pénètrent déjà dans la conscience avant même que surgit le désir ou la nécessité de s'occuper de leurs produits.» (VEGLA)

FAMILY SPORT

Energie-Versorgung Schwaben AG

GKN UNI-CARDAN AG
Ein Unternehmen der GKN Gruppe

AGENCE DE PROMOTION DES INVESTISSEMENTS API – TUNESIEN

DELTA

Corradini

M. Kübler & Sohn, seit 1908

Citroën.
Intelligenz auf Rädern.

ERICSSON

BANCA CATALANA

According to the Den Hague Convention to Protect Cultural Values of 1954, buildings and monuments marked by the blue and white sign (on the right) should "if possible" be spared during wars.

Nach der Haager Konvention zum Schutze von Kulturgut aus dem Jahre 1954 sollen mit dem blau-weissen Schild (rechts) gekennzeichnete Gebäude und Denkmäler im Krieg «nach Möglichkeit» geschont werden.

Selon la Convention sur la protection des biens culturels de La Haye (1954), tout bâtiment et tout monument marqué de l'insigne bleu-blanc (à droite) doit «autant que possible» être ménagé en cas de conflit armé.

 **BUCHTAL** QUALITÄTS-KERAMIK

 HITACHI

Club  Méditerranée

 Dresdner Bank

 **HOLLAND**

 PIONEER

Personalberatung Hermann Mark

 **JYSKE BANK**

Aer Lingus Der Luftweg nach Irland

 KENWOOD

 **Mink-Bürsten**

 National Westminster Bank

 kassel

 Virginia Commonwealth University

 SOLO Motormäher.

 Universität Essen Gesamthochschule

 SANYO

 GEA

 **UNIVERSITÄT KARLSRUHE**

 TUI

 NORTHWEST ORIENT

 Toskana-Umbrien

 The Bank of Tokyo, Ltd.

 UNITED TECHNOLOGIES PACKARD

 Pharmacia

 HERTIE

 TT-Saga-Line

 raak

Century Data Systems

 Mütter genesungswerk

 hosby haus

 **MONT BLANC**

43

Tenth Example

The handwriting can radiate a certain image: sympathy or antipathy. Exactly this handwriting—representative for us personally—tells much about the sender. The hand so-to-speak represents us.

Zehntes Beispiel

Die Handschrift schafft in ihrer Ausstrahlung ein bestimmtes Image: Sympathie oder Abneigung. Gerade das Schriftelement – stellvertretend für uns persönlich – verrät vieles vom Absender. Das Schriftbild vertritt uns quasi.

Dixième exemple

Par son rayonnement, l'écriture crée une certaine image qui engendre la sympathie ou l'antipathie. Elle est l'expression personnelle de celui qui écrit et révèle la personnalité de l'auteur. L'écriture est en quelque sorte l'image qui nous représente.

Some texts one does not like to read. Others create feelings of aesthetic elegance and balance. This qualitative effect wanders subconsciously into the imagination of the writer.
This is similar for typefaces and their typographic treatment.

Manche Texte mag man gar nicht lesen. Andere lösen Empfindungen von ästhetischer Eleganz und Ausgewogenheit aus. Diese Anmutungsqualität lassen wir unterbewusst in die Vorstellung über die Person des Schreibers einfliessen.
Ähnlich verhält es sich mit Satzlettern und der typografischen Aufbereitung.

Il y a des textes qu'on n'a guère envie de lire. D'autres produisent une impression esthétique d'élégance et d'harmonie, que l'on transpose inconsciemment sur la personne de l'auteur du texte.
Il en est de même pour les caractères de composition et la disposition typographique.

ZDF

All this in itself has nothing to do with the contents of what has been written. It is unpardonable, if the handwriting of a sender, the peculiarity of a corporate personality is softened by fashionable script games of inadequate typographic extravagances.

The example on this page shows, how this can manifest itself: Let's suppose that ZDF, one of the most highly frequented media in Germany, re-discovered the old script pen of my school years, it did not take long until this pen type was so much favoured that dozens of other graphic designers made use of it for other companies. We older graphic designers are familiar with the rise and fall of certain typefaces at two-year intervals: at one time it is Baskerville which "decorates" all advertisements, at another time bold Gill with the tiny little dot on the i.

A typographic institute in Frankfurt has looked at and investigated all typefaces of advertisements published in the "Spiegel" during the month of March 1982. Preferences are obvious.

In 42 advertisements the institute counted:

14 times Futura
 7 times Franklin Gothic
 6 times Helvetica
 4 times Times

(The others were miscellaneous, occurring once or twice each.)

You can see that Futura was "in" presently in Teutonia.

And there is the snag: if a new fashion comes up, the Art Director, in his next advertisement, will give a company a new typeface, the latest one en vogue.

But: consistency — and not adjustment to the graphic designer's taste — continuity for recognition are the prerequisites for personality. Also through the element of the typeface.

Das alles hat nichts mit dem Inhalt des Geschriebenen zu tun.

Es ist sträflich, wenn die Handschrift eines Absenders, die Eigenart der Persönlichkeit eines Unternehmens durch zeitmodische Schriftspielchen unadäquater Typomätzchen aufgeweicht wird.

Wie das aussehen kann, zeigt das Beispiel dieser Seite: Unterstellen wir, dass das ZDF als eines der meistkonsumierten Medien in Deutschland die alte Redisfederschrift meiner Schulzeit wiederentdeckte, so hat es nicht lang gedauert, bis diese Schriftart so beliebt wurde, dass die Grafiker gleich dutzendweise sich ihrer für andere Betriebe bemächtigten. Wir älteren Grafiker kennen dieses Aufkommen und Vergehen von Schriftvorlieben im Zweijahresrhythmus: Mal ist's die Baskerville, die alle Anzeigen «schmückt», mal die fette Gill mit dem mickrigen i-Punkt.

Ein Frankfurter Typostudio hat im Monat März 1982 alle Anzeigen des Magazins «Spiegel» auf Schrifttypen durchgesehen. Die Vorlieben sind deutlich.

Bei 42 Anzeigen zählten sie:

14mal Futura
 7mal Franklin Gothic
 6mal Helvetica
 4mal Times

(Der Rest waren verschiedene, je ein- oder zweimal.)

Man sieht, die Futura war grade mal wieder «in» bei Teutonen.

Und da ist eben der Haken: Kommt eine neue Mode auf, so wird der Art Director in seiner nächsten Anzeige der gleichen Firma eine andere Schrift verpassen, die gerade en vogue ist.

Aber: Konsequenz – und nicht Anpassung an Grafikergeschmack –, Kontinuität für Wiedererkennung ist Voraussetzung für die Personality. Auch durch das Element Schrift.

Tout cela n'a rien à voir avec le contenu.

Il est inadmissible de dénaturer l'écriture de l'«expéditeur» et, partant, les traits spécifiques de la personnalité d'une entreprise, par des fantaisies à la mode ou des extravagances typographiques inadéquates.

Si nous considérons que la deuxième chaîne allemande ZDF, un des médias les plus largement diffusés, a redécouvert l'ancienne écriture à la plume de mes années d'école, il n'a pas fallu longtemps jusqu'à ce que ce type de caractères connaisse partout une grande faveur. Les graphistes de ma génération connaissent ces phases bisannuelles d'engouement et de désaveu successifs lorsqu'il s'agit de choisir certains types de caractères: une fois c'est la Baskerville qui «orne» toutes les annonces, une autre fois, la Gill grasse avec le chétif point sur le i.

Un studio typographique de Francfort a examiné en mars 1982 toutes les annonces de la revue «Spiegel» pour établir les prédilections typographiques. Sur 42 annonces, ledit studio a compté:

14 fois Futura
 7 fois Franklin Gothic
 6 fois Helvetica
 4 fois Times

C'est là que réside précisément le problème: lorsqu'une nouvelle écriture à la mode fait son apparition, le directeur artistique s'empresse d'en faire étalage dans sa prochaine annonce pour la même entreprise.

Or: une personnalité d'entreprise exige une attitude conséquente (et non pas l'adaptation au goût d'un graphiste) et la continuité, garante de la reminiscence chez le destinataire. Les caractères typographiques y sont inclus comme éléments formels.

Eleventh Example

From looking at the previous example, the following can be derived:
Identity forms itself from the overall effect: Signet, typeface, typography, graphic elements, layout.
The unmistakable image is formed by the inter-action between message and appearance. Newspaper editors know this!

Elftes Beispiel

Aus der Betrachtung der vorigen Beispielseiten lässt sich ableiten:
Identity bildet sich aus der Gesamtanmutung. Aus der Summe der Details: Signet, Schrift, Typografie, grafische Elemente, Zusammenstellung.

Onzième exemple

Les exemples montrés sur les pages précédentes révèlent ce qui suit:
l'identité se dégage de la présentation globale de l'entreprise, de la somme des détails tels que sigle, caractères, typographie, éléments graphiques, composition.

Three typical representatives of a certain newspaper style are shown on this page. The overall image of the individual title pages, *on the basis of their outside appearance alone,* immediately lets us conclude what the style of the language and even the choice of subjects discussed is. Each of these three newspapers creates a definitive feeling in us.
Independently of how you personally judge upon the design: a clear identity evolves and contents and appearance are in conformity.

Das unverkennbare Erscheinungsbild wird aus dem Zusammenspiel von Botschaft und Aufmachung gebildet. Zeitungsredakteure wissen das!
Ich habe auf dieser Seite drei typische Vertreter eines bestimmten Zeitungsstils abgebildet. Das Gesamtbild der einzelnen Titelseiten lässt uns unmittelbar, *allein durch seine Aufmachung,* auch auf den Sprachstil und sogar die Gewichtung der Themenwahl schliessen. Die Anmutung dieser drei Zeitungen löst eine ganz bestimmte Empfindung aus.
Gleichgültig, wie Sie persönlich die Gestaltung bewerten: Es entsteht eine klare Identity, und der Inhalt und die Aufmachung entsprechen sich.

L'image d'entreprise clairement identifiable découle de la combinaison harmonieuse entre le message et sa présentation. Les rédacteurs de journaux connaissent bien ce principe!
L'image d'ensemble des pages de titre permet, *déjà par sa conception formelle,* de déduire quel est le style du texte et même la pondération attribuée aux thèmes choisis. Cette expression formelle des trois journaux déclenche une réaction déterminée.
Quelle que soit la valeur que l'on voudra bien lui accorder personnellement, la conception formelle engendre une identité claire et précise et établit une concordance entre le fond et la forme.

Now the typical design elements of three newspapers characteristics have been exchanged, and the "ruptures" between contents and appearance become obvious.

Admittedly, a game — but a conclusive one; because it can directly be related to CD. Such ruptures in the appearance of an enterprise can be found every day.

(This is demonstrated by the following seven sins against a closed CD.)

No newspaper could afford such slips, without irritating and thereby losing its readers. *It must maintain its identity all the way through.*

Jetzt sind die typischen Umbruchelemente der drei Zeitungscharakteristika ausgetauscht, und die «Brüche» von Inhalt zu Aufmachung werden deutlich.

Zugegeben, ein Spiel – aber ein aufschlussreiches; denn man kann es beispielhaft auf CD übertragen.

Solche Sprünge im Erscheinungsbild von Unternehmen sind alltäglich. (Die folgenden sieben Sünden wider ein geschlossenes CD demonstrieren das.)

Keine Zeitung könnte sich solche Ausrutscher leisten, ohne ihre Leser zu verunsichern und dadurch zu verlieren. *Sie muss ihre Identität durchhalten.*

Les éléments typiques de la mise en page des trois journaux ont maintenant été interchangés, et les «failles» entre le fond et la forme apparaissent clairement.

Certes, il s'agit d'un jeu, mais combien révélateur, car on peut par exemple le transposer en CD.

De telles fêlures sont fréquentes dans l'image d'identification d'une entreprise. (Les sept péchés contre un CD intégré le démontrent clairement.)

Aucun journal ne pourrait se permettre de telles bévues sans insécuriser ses lecteurs, voire même risquer de les perdre. *Il doit conserver son identité.*

Twelfth Example

Recognition and clear association with an enterprise can only come about on the basis of unmistakable characteristic features — especially if the logograms of the enterprise are as similar as the ones shown on this page.

Zwölftes Beispiel

Eine Wiedererkennung und eindeutige Zuordnung zum Unternehmen kann nur durch unverwechselbare Charakteristik entstehen – besonders wenn die Schriftzüge der Unternehmen sich so gleichen wie die auf dieser Seite aufgereihten.

Douzième exemple

La réminiscence et le «positionnement» clair de l'entreprise ne sont possibles que grâce à des caractéristiques excluant toute possibilité de confusion, surtout lorsque les logotypes des entreprises se ressemblent comme ceux «alignés» en série sur cette page.

BDF
DGB
RICOH
OSRAM
BOSCH
BASF
SABA
QUICK

In the experiment on these two pages, on the right-hand side I have only exchanged the logograms of actual advertisements, and in the three above the illustrations were mixed up in addition. You may draw your own conclusions from the results.
(After the startling similar resulting appearances), I will restrict myself to comparative quotes:
● "In communication identity signifies the sum of characteristics, which make a person or a group describable and definitely distinguishable."
(David J. de Levita)
● "… the public learns to recognize companies from definitive, unchanging features." (Roland Mielke)
● "… taking into account the multitude and the diversity of the Siemens product spectrum, it (advertising design) must at the same time signal the *one* sender of the many advertising messages,

Bei dem Experiment auf diesen beiden Seiten habe ich (rechts) nur die Schriftzüge von tatsächlichen Anzeigen ausgetauscht und bei den drei obenstehenden auch noch die Abbildungen durcheinandergewürfelt. Die Schlüsse aus dem Ergebnis mögen Sie selbst ziehen. Ich will mich (nach den frappierend ähnlichen Anmutungen) auf vergleichende Zitate beschränken:
● «Für die Kommunikation bedeutet Identität eine Summe von Kennzeichen, die eine Person oder Gruppe beschreibbar und exakt unterscheidbar machen.» (David J. de Levita)
● «… die Öffentlichkeit lernt, das Unternehmen an bestimmten, gleichbleibenden Merkmalen zu erkennen.» (Roland Mielke)
● «… soll sie (die werbliche Gestaltung) bei einer Vielzahl und Vielfalt des Siemens-Angebotsspektrums sogleich den *einen* Absender der vielen Werbebotschaften signalisieren,

Dans l'expérience présentée sur les deux pages ci-contre, j'ai simplement échangé (à droite) les logotypes d'annonces ayant effectivement parues; pour les trois logotypes (en haut), j'ai aussi interverti les reproductions. Je laisse au lecteur le soin de tirer lui-même les conclusions qui s'imposent. Je me bornerai (après les similitudes frappantes sur ces pages) à quelques citations invitant à la comparaison:
● «Pour la communication, l'identité signifie un ensemble de signes distinctifs qui permettent de décrire ou de distinguer avec précision une personne ou un groupe.»
(David J. de Levita)
● «… le public apprend à reconnaître l'entreprise d'après ses caractéristiques spécifiques invariables.»
(Roland Mielke)
● «… elle (la conception publicitaire) doit, face à la multiplicité et à la diversité de l'offre Siemens, signaler immédiatement l'expéditeur *unique* des nombreux messages publicitaires, …

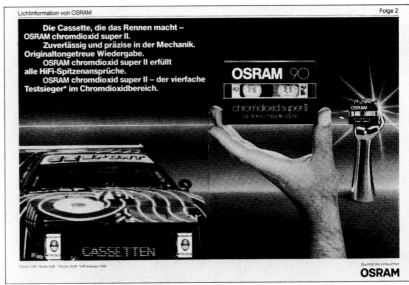

… 'the smallest, mutual, multiples' of
advertising design efforts are the
company symbol and the rules of the
game for its application …''
(G. Voment, ''So wirbt Siemens'')
● ''Garments make people: the company personality presents itself
through its appearance, the 'corporate
design'…''
(K. Birkigt / M. Stadler)
● ''A company appearance, in which
all visuals and measures are coordi-
nated, cannot only be recognized faster, it also has a higher memory.''
(A. Stankowski, ''Corporate Identity'')
● ''Each advertisement should be
considered a contribution to the
image.'' (Dr. F. Eichler)

… ‹kleinstes gemeinsames Vielfa-
ches› werblicher Gestaltungsarbeit
sind das Firmensymbol und die Spielregeln für dessen Anwendung …»
(G. Voment, «So wirbt Siemens»)
● «Kleider machen Leute: Die Unternehmenspersönlichkeit stellt sich dar
in ihrem Erscheinungsbild, dem ‹corporate design› …»
(K. Birkigt / M. Stadler)
● «Ein Firmenbild, in dem alle Visuells
und Masse aufeinander abgestimmt
sind, ist nicht nur schneller wieder-
zuerkennen, es hat auch einen höhe-
ren Behaltewert.»
(A. Stankowski, «Corporate Identity»)
● «Jede Anzeige sollte als Beitrag
zum Image betrachtet werden.»
(Dr. F. Eichler)

… la plus petite forme d'expression du
travail créatif commun, aux facettes si
variées, est le symbole de l'entreprise
et les règles de jeu régissant son
application…» (G. Voment dans
«Siemens et la publicité»)
● «Même si le proverbe dit que
l'«habit ne fait pas le moine», la personnalité de l'entreprise s'exprime par
son image d'identification, par le «corporate design»…»
(K. Birkigt / M. Stadler)
● «L'image d'entreprise qui combine
harmonieusement tous les éléments
visuels et toutes les dimensions est
non seulement plus rapidement
reconnaissable, mais possède une
plus grande valeur de réminiscence.»
(A. Stankowski, «Corporate Identity»)
● «Chaque annonce devrait être
considérée comme une contribution à
l'image de l'entreprise.» (F. Eichler)

Derived from the previous examples, and my own rules and regulations, for clarification an anti-catalogue against a closed CD follows:

Seven good ways to serve heterogenity—seven offences against individuality and CI.

Abgeleitet von den vorausgegangenen zwölf Beispielen, meinen aufgestellten Regeln und Thesen, folgt zur Verdeutlichung ein Antikatalog gegen eine geschlossene CD.

Sieben gute Möglichkeiten zur Pflege von Heterogenität – sieben Verstösse wider Eigenständigkeit und eine CI.

Dérivé des douze exemples présentés plus haut, ainsi que des thèses et règles déjà énoncées, voici l'«anti-catalogue» d'un CD intégré.

Sept excellentes possibilités pour perpétuer une image hétérogène – sept fautes contre le profil spécifique de l'entreprise et la CI

First sin: impersonal appearance
● The surrealistic showings of the same make wipe out all company-specific individuality.

Erste Sünde: Unpersönlichkeit
● Diese surrealistischen Darstellungen gleicher Machart verwischen jede firmenspezifische Eigentümlichkeit.

Premier péché: le manque de personnalité
● Quelle que soit leur conception formelle, ces représentations surréalistes estompent toute caractéristique spécifique à l'entreprise.

Second sin: ego trips
- Individual product competence in delegated responsibility
- Diversification and resulting varying "subsidiary profiles"
- Independent appearances in the markets (folcloristic adjustment)

Zweite Sünde: Ego-Tips
- Einzelproduktzuständigkeit in delegierter Verantwortung
- Diversifikation und daraus folgend verschiedene «subsidiary-profiles»
- Sologestaltung der Auftritte in den Märkten (folkloristische Anpassung)

Deuxième péché: les «ego-trips»
- Compétence pour un produit par délégation de la responsabilité
- Diversification et «subsidiary-profiles» qui en découlent
- Conception «solo» des présentations sur les divers marchés

Third sin: inconsistencies
● Measuring success of the "campaign" only from sales, not considering long-term effects
● Abandoning the established identity in the event of market difficulties

Dritte Sünde: Unstetigkeit
● Erfolgsmessen einer «Kampagne» nur am Umsatz ohne Berücksichtigung der Langzeitwirkung
● Verlassen der etablierten Identity bei Marktschwierigkeiten

Troisième péché: l'instabilité
● Evaluation du succès d'une «campagne» d'après le seul chiffre d'affaires, sans considérer l'effet à long terme
● Abandon de l'identité établie dès que le marché présente des difficultés

The Chairman of a large Japanese company said the following (analogously): "As long as in the United States there is Wall Street with its shareholders, nothing can happen to us Japanese: we invest into the future. If we don't make profit right away and later on only break even, we will certainly dominate the *entire* market within the next few years."
And so it happened with cameras, Hifi and video appliances, and motor bicycles.
How did Opel think of this in its promotion of Rekord and Ascona, when the medium-size cars were suffering during the time of increasing gas prices? What effect has such selling-out on the reputation, on the image of the other Opel models?

Vom Vorsitzenden eines grossen japanischen Unternehmens ist der Ausspruch bekanntgeworden (sinngemäss): «Solange es in Amerika die Wall Street mit Ihren Aktionären gibt, kann uns Japanern nichts passieren: Haben wir nicht gleich Profit, dann dominieren wir sicher den *ganzen* Markt in kommenden Jahren.»
So geschehen bei Kameras, HiFi- und Videogeräten, Motorrädern.
Wie Opel das wohl bei seiner Promotion für Rekord und Ascona bedachte, als es den Mittelklassewagen im Laufe der Benzinverteuerung schlecht ging? Welche Auswirkung hat solch Ausverkauf auf die Reputation, auf das Image und die übrigen Opel-Modelle?

Le directeur d'une grande entreprise japonaise a dit en substance: «Aussi longtemps qu'il existe aux Etats-Unis la Wall Street avec ses actionnaires, nous, les Japonais, nous n'avons rien à redouter: si nous n'atteignons pas immédiatement le bénéfice escompté, mais seulement le ‹seuil de rentabilité›, alors nous sommes sûrs de dominer la *totalité* du marché l'année suivante.
C'est ce qui s'est passé pour les caméras, appareils hifi, enregistreurs vidéo, motocyclettes.
Qu'a bien pu penser Opel dans sa promotion pour Rekord et Ascona lors de la crise du pétrole? Et quelle est l'incidence de telles «ventes au rabais» sur la réputation, l'image des autres modèles Opel?

52

Fourth sin: fashion-hunting

● Unorganic typographical typeface cocktail

In the majority of cases the so-called customer taste is only an excuse for one's own bad taste.

Fifth sin: poverty of ideas

● Acceptance of advertising tricks
● Missing individuality and affirmative copying of "success recepies"
● Missing initiative; pursuing so-called consumer expectancies

In the example below, detailed deliberation is required to determine whether tobacco or jeans are meant. A typical advertising agency style has developed; producer identification is hard to achieve.

Vierte Sünde: Geschmäcklerei

● Unorganischer typografischer Schriftsalat

In den meisten Fällen ist der soge-nannte Kundengeschmack nur Ent-schuldigung für den schlechten eige-nen.

Fünfte Sünde: Einfallslosigkeit

● Einschwenken auf Werbemaschen
● Mangelnde Eigenständigkeit und affirmatives Übernehmen von «Erfolgsrezepten»
● Mangelnde Eigeninitiative; soge-nannten Konsumentenerwartungen nachlaufend

Bei den untenstehenden Beispielen lässt sich nur nach eingehender Betrachtung feststellen, ob Tabak oder Jeans gemeint sind. Es ist ein typischer Werbeagenturstil entstan-den, eine Produzentenzuordnung ist nur schwer möglich.

Quatrième péché: le mauvais goût

● Incohérence et discordance dans la présentation typographique

Dans la plupart des cas, le prétendu goût des clients n'est qu'une piètre excuse pour son mauvais goût per-sonnel.

Cinquième péché: le manque d'imagination

● Emballement pour des «gags» publicitaires en vogue
● Manque de personnalité et adop-tion spontanée de «recettes promet-teuses de succès»
● Initiative personnelle déficiente; course aux «expectations des consommateurs» à satisfaire

Dans les exemples présentés ci-des-sous, il faut un effort soutenu pour découvrir s'il s'agit de tabac ou de jeans. Le style est typique pour une agence de publicité, la référence au produit est difficile à déceler.

Sixth sin: no coherence
- The CD elements fall apart: PR, promotion and advertising differ

Sechste Sünde: Inkonsequenz
- Die Faktoren des CD fallen auseinander: PR, Promotion und Werbung sind unterschiedlich

Sixième péché: l'inconséquence
- Les éléments constitutifs du CD perdent leur cohésion: RP, promotion et publicité divergent

---

Seventh sin: ''borrowed interest''
- Identity dislocation due to bare-breasted and sparkling beauties
- Product image and communication do not correspond

Siebte Sünde: «borrowed interest»
- Identity-Verschiebung durch barbusige oder popige Schönheiten
- Produktanmutung und Kommunikation entsprechen sich nicht

Septième péché: les «borrowed interests»
- Altération de l'identité par des beautés semi-voilées ou «pop»
- La présentation du produit et la communication ne concordent pas

On the previous five pages CD criteria were shown, which may result from seven sins (certainly there are others). In conclusion, seven hypothetical individuals, who may cause a collapse of CD, are shown:

Seven "CI sinners"

1. A square-box graphic designer,
who, with rigid rules, dictatorships and "thoughtless repeating of recipes" according to the "graphic standard manual" suffocates every natural development.

2. A so-called successful "CI agency",
which is bound to be primarily concerned with a chic CD creation; which, however, has to sell itself to the customer primarily on the basis of orgiastic ideas.

3. A marketing manager determined by sales curves,
to whom identity and roundedness are uncomfortable, because they don't voluntarily bend to his "actions": "job rotating" determines the design.

4. A capricious Creative Director,
who primarily presents *himself or his agency,* and to whom the company image is in the way. The artist's handwriting determines CD.

5. An advertising manager,
within whom the concept of Corporate Identity creates the commonplace visions of provincial advertising.

6. A new manager,
who does not want to have anything to do with the profile created by his predecessor and who for that reason possibly starts with firing the ones responsible and changes the agency.

7. An unsecure management,
which, on the basis of an expansion just as in the event of a recession, replaces the soul of the company with a bloodless "new identity".

Auf den fünf Seiten zuvor sind durch sieben Sünden denkbare CD-Kriterien aufgezeigt (sicher gibt es auch andere). Abschliessend sieben hypothetische Verursacher eines CD-Kollapses.

Sieben «CI-Sünder»

1. Ein Raster-Schachtel-Grafiker,
der mit starren Regeln, Festschreibungen und «Abziehen von Rezepten» nach «graphic standard manuals» jede lebendige Entfaltung erstickt.

2. Eine sogenannt erfolgreiche «CI-Agentur»,
der es in erster Linie darum gehen muss, eine schicke CD-Creation zu schaffen. Die sich aber vorrangig selbst durch orgiastische Ideen an einen Kunden verkaufen muss.

3. Ein von Umsatzkurven bestimmter Marketing-Manager,
dem Identity und Geschlossenheit unbequem sind, weil sie sich seinen «Aktionen» nicht willfährig beugen: «Job-rotating» bestimmt die Gestaltung.

4. Ein eigensinniger Creative Director,
der zuallererst *sich selbst oder seine Agentur darstellt* und dem das Herstellerbild eher störend im Wege ist. Die Handschrift des «Künstlers» bestimmt das CD.

5. Ein Werbeleiter,
für den der Begriff Corporate Identity die biederen Vorstellungen provinzieller Reklame auslöst.

6. Ein neuer Manager,
der mit dem Profil, das sein Vorgänger geschaffen hat, nichts anfangen will. Der als erstes die Linienverantwortlichen feuert und die Agentur wechselt.

7. Ein unsicheres Management,
das aufgrund von Expansion genauso wie Umsatzrückgang eine blutarme «neue» Identity vor die Seele des Unternehmens stellt.

Les cinq pages précédentes ont permis de suggérer – par le truchement des sept péchés – quelques critères CD déterminants (il en existe certainement d'autres). Pour conclure, voici sept responsables hypothétiques d'un «effondrement» du CD.

Sept «pécheurs CI»

1. Le graphiste entiché de schémas et de trames
qui, par des règles figées, des prescriptions inflexibles, la reproduction servile de «recettes» étouffe tout épanouissement spontané.

2. L'«agence CI» soi-disant réputée
qui s'applique, en première ligne, à créer un CD raffiné, mais qui doit tout d'abord se vendre elle-même à un client par des idées «orgiastiques».

3. Le directeur de marketing rivé à ses courbes sur le chiffre d'affaires
et que l'identité et la cohérence de la «personnality» incommodent parce qu'elles ne se plient pas sans autre à ses exigences: la «job rotation» détermine la conception formelle.

4. Le directeur d'art capricieux
qui *se présente d'abord lui-même ou son agence,* et qui ressent l'image du producteur comme plutôt perturbatrice. C'est la signature de l'«artiste» qui détermine le CD.

5. Le directeur de publicité
pour qui le terme de Corporate Identity évoque les formes étriquées de la réclame provinciale.

6. Le nouveau «manager»
qui se distancie sciemment du profil créé par son prédécesseur, qui commence par se débarrasser des responsables en ligne et change d'agence de publicité.

7. La direction indécise
et qui, en raison de l'expansion de l'entreprise et de la régression du chiffre d'affaires, préfère une nouvelle identité «anémique» à l'âme de l'entreprise.

Sie kommen, unterschreiben und fahren ab.

"You come, sign and depart."
«Vous arrivez, signez et repartez.»

"The advertising manager and the designer are confronted with the difficult and responsible task …
… to find artistically appealing solutions of his drafts …'' (Dr. J. A. Thuma)

"Just as technical innovation and commercial management require independent persons, the innovation of new soulful design expressions requires much artistic strength, artistic personality." (Gropius)

«Der Werbeleiter und der Werbegestalter stehen vor der schwierigen und verantwortungsvollen Aufgabe …
… künstlerisch ansprechende Lösungen seiner Entwürfe zu finden …»
(Dr. J. A. Thuma)

«Genauso wie technische Erfindung und kaufmännische Regie selbständige Köpfe verlangen, fordert die Erfindung neuer beseelter Formausdrücke starke Künstlerkraft, künstlerische Persönlichkeit.» (Gropius)

«Le directeur de la publicité et le créateur publicitaire sont confrontés à des tâches difficiles, lourdes de responsabilités...
... consistant à trouver des solutions artistiques à leurs projets...»
(J. A. Thuma)

«Tout comme les inventions techniques et la gestion commerciale exigent des esprits forts, de même l'invention de nouvelles formes d'expression créatrices requièrent la force vive et la personnalité de l'artiste.»
(Gropius)

Design
Standards
Manual

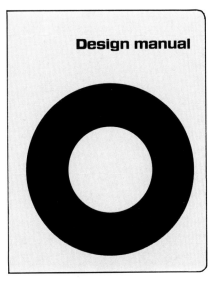

Design manual

Design-Manual

8×4

Centrale
Marketinggesellschaft
der deutschen
Agrarwirtschaft
m.b.H.

Gestaltungsrichtlinien

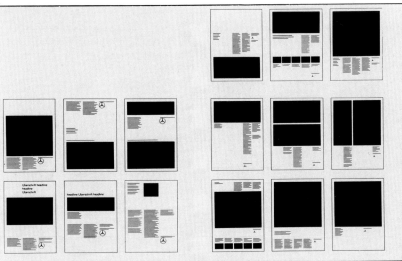

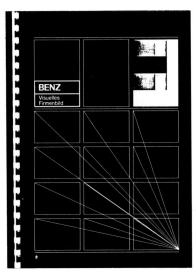

BENZ
Visuelles
Firmenbild

Identification
Guidelines

Internal Revenue Service

Internal Revenue Service

''Of course, just this important subject of 'Corporate Identity' has experienced such a scientific treatment that business managements of medium-size and small enterprises, feel revoked rather than appealed by the fuss that some advertising circles make in this field.'' (Ralph Schneider)

«Allerdings ist gerade dieses wichtige Thema ‹Corporate Identity› einer derartigen Verwissenschaftlichung zum Opfer gefallen, dass sich Geschäftsleitungen eher abgestossen fühlten von dem Rummel, den einige Kreise der Werbewirtschaft hier entfacht hatten.» (Ralph Schneider)

«Il est vrai que précisément le thème très important de la ‹Corporate Identity› est devenu la proie d'un tel acharnement scientifique que la direction des petites et moyennes entreprises se sent plutôt rebutée qu'attirée par le tapage déclenché par certains protagonistes de la publicité.»
(R. Schneider)

57

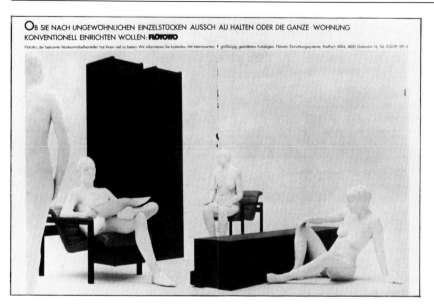

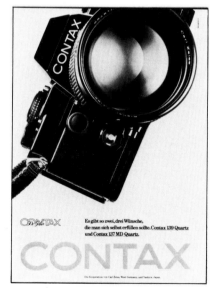

''We have developed a new species of advertisers, who are less interested in the product than in profits.'' (Jerry Della Femina)

«Wir haben eine neue Art von Werbern entwickelt, die weniger am Produkt, sondern mehr am Gewinn interessiert sind.» (Jerry Della Femina)

«Nous avons développé une nouvelle sorte de publicitaires, intéressés beaucoup moins au produit qu'au profit réalisé.» (Jerry Della Femina)

"The root of all creative work is in a human evaluation of the consumer. It is unexplainable, how rather nice and intelligent people can otherwise believe, that something functions in an advertisement, which in a human being they would think of as absurd, presumptious, belied or despicable." (Helmut Schmitz)

«Die Wurzel aller kreativen Arbeit liegt in einer menschenwürdigen Einschätzung des Verbrauchers. Es ist unerklärlich, wie sonst ganz nette und intelligente Menschen glauben können, dass etwas in einer Anzeige funktioniert, was sie bei einem Menschen albern, unbescheiden, dümmlich, verlogen oder verächtlich finden würden.» (Helmut Schmitz)

«La racine de tout travail créateur réside dans l'appréciation du consommateur en pleine conscience de sa dignité humaine. Il est inexplicable comment des hommes, parfaitement agréables et intelligents par ailleurs, s'imaginent que dans une annonce quelque chose puisse fonctionner qu'ils taxeraient de naïf, prétentieux, sot, mensonger ou méprisant chez l'homme.» (Helmut Schmitz)

"The aspects of 'style' and 'identity' are essentially interwoven. Because: The Corporate Identity determines the entire communicative appearance. On the other hand, at the same time it is true: He, who is inventive with regard to style, is no fool otherwise."
(H. D. Dahlhoff / P. Maeschig)

«Die Aspekte von ‹Stil› und ‹Identität› sind wesentlich miteinander verknüpft. Denn: Die Corporate Identity bestimmt den Stil des gesamten kommunikativen Auftretens. Andererseits gilt ebenso: Wer sich im Stil etwas einfallen lässt, ist auch sonst nicht auf den Kopf gefallen.»
(H.D. Dahlhoff / P. Maeschig)

«Les aspects du ‹style› et de l'‹identité› sont étroitement liés dans leur essence profonde. Car: la Corporate Identity détermine le style de l'ensemble de la présentation communicative. D'autre part, il est bien vrai que celui qui est à même de développer des idées originales dans le style, n'est pas non plus tombé sur la tête par ailleurs.»
(H.D. Dahlhoff / P. Maeschig)

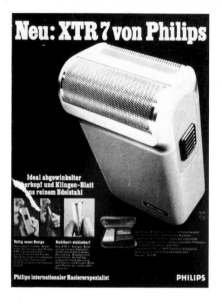

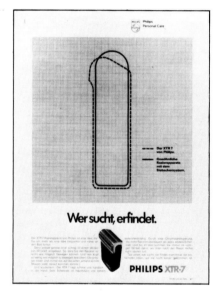

Philips Film Slogan:

"Simply years ahead"

Philips-Film-Slogan:
«Simply years ahead» (übersetzt: «Einfach um Jahre voraus»).

Slogan d'un film Philips:
«Simply years ahead»
(Tout simplement des années d'avance)

Conclusive and Transitional Remarks

It has taken a little more than two years to write this first part of the book. In the years preceding I have collected and assorted the documentation. The individual paragraphs were again and again tackled anew, modified, refined, supplemented, newly illustrated or rewritten. Often whole chapters disappeared again and were replaced by more pertaining examples. Had not the date of issue been firm, I would still continue to work on it!

The subject is so manifold — new experiences and knowledge are collected continuously — that to be honest, I should not close the subject: how is our advertising going to be in two years?

In an advertisement from Telefunken — propaganda so to speak — it reads verbatimly: ''Klaus, come on out and look at the stupid spot on television.'' If advertisers write something like this themselves …

Maybe this helps to explain why I have complained so much. But above all I had to criticize, that there is not one Corporate Design for all advertising. Possibly, however, the very reason why so many examples of negative impact have been presented (as they cannot be seen otherwise in such quantity and composition) is that I compared them systematically.

I had started from very high expectations and ideals.

Abschliessende und überleitende Bemerkung

Die Arbeit an diesem ersten Teil des Buches hat etwas mehr als zwei Jahre gedauert. Die Jahre davor habe ich das Material gesammelt und zusammengestellt. Die einzelnen Abschnitte wurden immer wieder neu angepackt, umgestellt, verfeinert, ergänzt, neu bebildert oder umgeschrieben. Oft sind Kapitel dann wieder ganz rausgeflogen und durch sinnfälligere Belege ersetzt worden. Wäre nicht der Erscheinungstermin festgesetzt gewesen, ich glaube, ich würde heute noch daran weitermachen!

Das Thema ist so vielschichtig – ständig kommen neue Erfahrungen und Einsichten dazu –, dass ich die Thematik, will ich ehrlich sein, gar nicht abschliessen dürfte: Wie sieht denn unsere Werbung in zwei Jahren aus?

In einer Anzeige von Telefunken – also in Reklame sozusagen – steht wörtlich: «Klaus, komm raus und sieh dir bloss mal wieder diese blöde Reklame im Fernsehen an.» Wenn Werber so etwas schon selbst schreiben …

Vielleicht ist so mit erklärlich, warum ich soviel verrissen habe. Aber vor allem fand ich zu kritisieren, dass ein Corporate Design für alle Reklame nicht existiert. Möglicherweise sind auch nur deshalb soviel Beispiele negativer Ausprägung konfrontiert (wie sie sonst in dieser Fülle und Zusammenstellung nicht zu sehen sind), weil ich sie systematisch verglich.

Ich war von einer ganz hohen Erwartung und Idealvorstellung ausgegangen.

Remarques de conclusion et de transition

La préparation de cette première partie du présent ouvrage a duré plus de deux ans. Auparavant, j'ai collectionné et ordonné le matériel documentaire. Les différents passages ont été constamment reconsidérés, remaniés, précisés, complétés, restructurés et récrits. Souvent des chapitres entiers ont été biffés et remplacés par des contributions plus adéquates. Sans la date limite imposée par la parution du présent ouvrage, je crois que j'y travaillerai aujourd'hui encore!

Le sujet est si varié (de nouvelles connaissances et expériences s'y ajoutent constamment) que vouloir en donner une vue exhaustive équivaut à une véritable gageure: car, comment se présentera notre publicité d'ici deux ans?

Dans une annonce de Telefunken, il est dit textuellement: «Klaus, viens vite voir cette stupide réclame qui passe de nouveau à la télé.» Que dire, si même les publicitaires écrivent pareille chose…!

Peut-être comprendra-t-on maintenant mieux pourquoi j'ai remis en question tant de choses et pourquoi je critique l'absence de tout Corporate Design dans tant de réclames. Si tant d'exemples à caractère négatif sont réunis ici (en un nombre et en une variété rarement atteints ailleurs), c'est sans doute dû à mon effort systématique de comparaison et de confrontation.

J'étais parti d'expectations et de conceptions idéalistes très élevées.

When I leafed through the completed book layout for the first time, I was somewhat frightened. My good friends, to whom I gave it to read, it is true, thought that everything was correct. One even thought it was "over-whelmingly expressive". But they also asked, what can the graphic designer, the advertising man, the marketing man do now, if he does not want to fall into one of the traps discussed? Does not one always offend something or other?

They advised me to at least in the twelve examples present more *positive* attempts. I thought about it and dismissed the idea.

First of all, the negative examples appear to me to speak a clearer language. "You must *not...*"was written in the ten recommendations. What should not be done, is known. More-over, if just turned around, they are instructions.

Second, I said it at the beginning: usually in this kind of illustrated books, we are just shown the raisins in the cake. We'll see these now, too! Eight case studies shall prove that there are pathes that can be followed — and even that these pathes lead to higher respect and business success, and that they speak for themselves.

Als ich das Buchlayout im ganzen erstmals durchblättern konnte, bin ich doch etwas erschrocken. Meine guten Freunde, denen ich es zu lesen gab, fanden zwar alles richtig. Ja einer sogar «überwältigend eindrucksvoll». Aber sie fragten auch, was man denn nun als Grafiker, als Werbemann, als Marketing-Verantwortlicher eigentlich noch tun könne, wolle man nicht in irgendeinen der besprochenen Fehler verfallen. Gegen irgend etwas ver-stösst man doch immer?

Sie haben mir zugeraten, doch wenig-stens bei den zwölf Beispielen mehr *positive* Ansätze aufzuzeigen. Ich habe schon überlegt und habe es dann doch gelassen.

Erstens scheinen mir die Negativmu-ster eine deutlichere Sprache zu spre-chen. «Du sollst *nicht...*» war schon bei den Zehn Geboten geschrieben. Man weiss, was man nicht machen soll. Im übrigen braucht man sie nur genau umzudrehen, um eine Anlei-tung darin zu sehen.

Zweitens, ich sagte es eingangs schon: Üblicherweise bekommen wir in dieser Art Bilderbücher immer nur die Rosinen aus dem Kuchen serviert. Die kommen jetzt auch!

Acht Fallstudien sollen belegen, dass es doch gangbare Wege gibt – ja dass diese Wege zu höherem Ansehen und Geschäftserfolg führen, sie für sich sprechen.

Lorsque j'ai feuilleté pour la première fois le layout du présent ouvrage dans son ensemble, j'ai été quelque peu effrayé. Mes amis, auxquels j'ai donné à lire mon manuscrit, trouvaient que tout ce que je disais était juste. L'un d'eux estimait même que c'était «fort impressionnant». Mais ils ont égale-ment demandé ce qu'il convenait maintenant de faire en tant que gra-phiste, publicitaire, responsable du marketing, pour ne pas tomber dans l'une ou l'autre des erreurs déjà décri-tes. Car, quoi que l'on fasse, n'est-il pas vrai qu'on s'inscrit toujours en faux contre quelque chose?

Mes amis m'ont conseillé de montrer du moins davantage d'aspects *posi-tifs.* Après avoir longuement réfléchi, j'ai décidé de ne rien changer.

D'abord, les modèles négatifs me paraissent beaucoup plus éloquents. «Tu ne dois *pas...*» disent déjà les 10 commandements. Il suffit d'ailleurs de retourner les exemples négatifs pour en dégager des instructions positives.

Ensuite: les ouvrages illustrés traitant ce genre de problèmes présentent souvent uniquement des exemples de prestige.

De tels exemples prestigieux ne sau-raient manquer ici!

Huit études de cas apporteront la preuve qu'il existe des solutions qui mènent finalement plus haut et à de meilleurs résultats financiers, qui par-lent un langage clair et percutant.

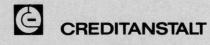 **CREDITANSTALT**

Design: Studio Schmittel
in cooperation with:
- CA Advertising Department
- Klaus Reisinger
- Advertising Agency "Die Sieber"

Design: Atelier Schmittel,
unter Mitwirkung von:
- Werbeabteilung CA
- Klaus Reisinger
- Werbeagentur «Die Sieber»

Design: Atelier Schmittel
en coopération avec:
- département de publicité CA
- Klaus Reisinger
- Agence de publicité «Die Sieber»

The Creditanstalt was founded in 1855. From the very start it has been closely connected with the Austrian economy, and it has made a large contribution to the economic recovery of the country after World War II.
The Creditanstalt is a respectable and responsible enterprise, and at the same time it is very dynamic.
Towards 1971 due to its expansive policies the main building of the bank was short of room, which had a negative effect especially on EDP. The Board therefore decided to build a Technical Center. This building today is part of the expression of CA's self-comprehension.
The growth of the bank and its penetration of new customer circles made it necessary for CA to represent itself more forcibly towards the outside, without, at that time, uniform design guidelines.
This created a multitude of communicative approaches, behind which the original company image almost disappeared altogether. Therefore, a consistent appearance typical of the CA was developed, which made it possible for the customer and employee to identify themselves with the bank.
From basic advertising means to architecture, i.e. in all aspects of communication this appearance is in conformity with the image of an internationally successful bank.

Die Creditanstalt wurde 1855 gegründet. Sie ist mit Österreichs Wirtschaft, vor allem der Industrie, von Beginn an auf das engste verknüpft und hat zum wirtschaftlichen Wiederaufbau des Landes nach dem Zweiten Weltkrieg einen wichtigen Beitrag geleistet. Sie ist ein solides, verantwortungsbewusstes Unternehmen, gleichzeitig aber auch eine Bank voller Dynamik.
Durch die expansive Entwicklung entstanden gegen 1971 im Hauptgebäude räumliche Engpässe, die besonders die Arbeit der EDV beeinträchtigten. Deshalb beschloss der Vorstand den Bau eines technischen Zentrums. Dieses Gebäude ist heute Teil des Ausdruckes des CA-Selbstverständnisses.
Mit dem Wachstum der Bank und ihrem Vordringen in neue Kundenschichten musste die CA verstärkt in der Öffentlichkeit präsentiert werden, ohne dass aber einheitliche gestalterische Richtlinien existierten. So entstand eine unüberschaubare Vielfalt von kommunikativen Ansprecharten, hinter denen der ursprüngliche Firmencharakter fast verschwand. Deshalb wurde ein der CA entsprechendes, konsequentes Erscheinungsprofil entwickelt, das Kunden und Mitarbeitern die Voraussetzungen zur Identifikation mit der Bank gibt. Es entspricht in allen Kommunikationsformen von den eigentlichen Werbemitteln bis zur Architektur dem Image einer international erfolgreichen Bank.

La Creditanstalt a été fondée en 1855. Dès le départ, elle a été étroitement associée à l'économie et, plus particulièrement, à l'industrie de l'Autriche. Après la Seconde Guerre mondiale, elle a fourni une importante contribution au redressement du pays.
La Creditanstalt est une entreprise solide, consciente de ses responsabilités, tout en étant une banque pleine de dynamisme.
La politique d'expansion a abouti vers 1971 à un manque flagrant de place dans le bâtiment principal, entravant tout particulièrement le travail du secteur informatique. Pour cette raison, le Comité de direction a décidé la construction d'un centre technique. Cet immeuble forme aujourd'hui partie intégrante de l'identité CA.
Avec la croissance de la banque et sa pénétration dans de nouvelles couches de clients, il importait de mettre davantage en valeur l'image CA aux yeux du public. Ainsi a été créée une infinie variété d'éléments graphiques derrière lesquels le caractère original de l'entreprise s'estompait littéralement. Pour cette raison, un profil d'identification conséquent, spécifique à la CA, a été développé dans le but de faciliter l'identification des clients et des collaborateurs avec la banque. Dans toutes les formes de communication, depuis les moyens publicitaires jusqu'à l'architecture, ce profil correspond à l'image d'une banque opérant avec succès sur le plan international.

Technical Center Vienna   **Technisches Zentrum Wien**   **Le Centre technique à Vienne**

The TC is a symbol of transparency, human open-mindedness and actuality, which has always been our goal. The Technical Center has not just become a mere office building, but — due to the direct connections to the Department Store, etc.— it was integrated into an existing social environment. In its design, the CA gave much thought to its municipal responsibilities.

On the premises of the old Franz-Joseph-Railway Station in Vienna a building was set up that leaves room for 2200 CA employees, for EDP, as well as for the new Railway Station, a department store, a CA branch, a police station and various business premises; a parking house is connected to the main building.

The size of the building made it necessary to create an easily understandable orientation system, and this was achieved by four "different color" areas with matching doors and reference signs.

Das TZ steht als Symbol für die Transparenz, menschliche Aufgeschlossenheit und Aktualität, die wir in unserer Bank immer angestrebt haben. Das technische Zentrum ist nicht ein reines Bürogebäude geworden, sondern wurde – zum Beispiel durch die direkte Verbindung mit dem Kaufhaus usw. – in ein vorhandenes soziales Umfeld eingefügt. Die CA war sich bei der Ausgestaltung ihrer städtebaulichen Verpflichtung bewusst.

Auf dem Gelände des alten Franz-Joseph-Bahnhofs entstand ein Gebäude, das Platz bietet für 2200 Mitarbeiter der CA, für die EDV sowie für den neuen Bahnhof, ein Kaufhaus, eine CA-Filiale, eine Polizeiwachstube und verschiedene Geschäftslokale; angeschlossen an das Hauptgebäude ist eine Parkgarage.

Die Grösse des Gebäudes machte die Entwicklung eines leicht verständlichen Orientierungssystems nötig, was durch die Einteilung in vier «farbverschiedene» Bereiche mit entsprechenden Tür- und Hinweisschildern gelöst wurde.

CT est le symbole de qualités que notre banque a toujours hautement appréciées: transparence, ouverture d'esprit aux problèmes humains et actualité. Le Centre technique n'est pas simplement un immeuble administratif, mais – en raison de ses relations directes avec le grand-magasin, par exemple – il est intégré à l'environnement social existant. La CA a développé la conception du CT en pleine conscience de ses responsabilités sur le plan de l'aménagement urbain.

Sur le terrain de l'ancienne gare Franz-Joseph, un immeuble a été construit qui abrite les 2200 collaborateurs de la CA, le département informatique, ainsi que la nouvelle gare, une succursale CA, un poste de police et divers locaux commerciaux; un parking est directement rattaché au bâtiment principal.

Les dimensions des bâtiments ont rendu nécessaire la création d'un système d'orientation facile à comprendre. Ce but a été atteint grâce à la subdivision en quatre secteurs de couleurs différentes, avec les écriteaux sur les portes et les panneaux indicateurs correspondants.

Our Motivations

Unsere Beweggründe

Nos motifs d'agir

During the sixties and seventies, economic structures changed as dramatically as never before.

The CA developed the most manifold appearances due to the ever-increasing number of branch outlets and the diversity of necessary correspondence. From the standpoint of the individual departments, these solutions were all usable and justified; however, the person on the outside must have had difficulties in discovering *his* CA in all of these variations. Institutions as the CA are in need of definitive styling elements in order to convincingly present the special character of their personality; because the picture the public forms of the CA — its respect and its reputation — is essentially determined by the quality of its visual appearance. This is from which the outsider derives the bank's competence and its economic standing.

If a bank wants to convince its customers, the prerequisite is reliability and professional competence in business life. A uniform system of communication in all areas enables the customer to recognize these qualities in a bank.

Each contact between one of our employees and a customer should be backed by a clear and unequivocal picture of the CA: that of a dynamic, cosmopolitan, large bank of international character.

Während der sechziger und siebziger Jahre änderte sich die geschäftliche Struktur so entscheidend wie nie zuvor. Bedingt durch die steigende Anzahl der Filialen und die Vielfalt des notwendigen Schriftverkehrs, entwikkelten sich die verschiedenartigsten Darstellungsformen für die CA. Diese Lösungen waren – von der jeweiligen Abteilung aus gesehen – alle brauchbar und begründet, doch dem Aussenstehenden musste es schwerfallen, hinter allen Variationen sofort *seine* CA zu erkennen.

Institutionen wie die CA brauchen bestimmte Stilelemente, um das Besondere ihrer Persönlichkeit überzeugend darzustellen; denn das Bild, das die Öffentlichkeit von der CA hat – ihr Ansehen und ihr Ruf –, wird wesentlich von der Qualität des visuellen Erscheinungsbildes geprägt. Ihre Kompetenz, ja sogar ihre Marktbedeutung werden vom Aussenstehenden daraus abgeleitet.

Will eine Bank ihre Kunden überzeugen, ist die Voraussetzung dafür Zuverlässigkeit und fachliche Kompetenz im Geschäftsleben. Ein geschlossenes System der Kommunikation in allen Bereichen ermöglicht dem Kunden, diese Qualitäten einer Bank zu erkennen.

Deshalb sollte hinter jeder Kontaktaufnahme zwischen einem unserer Mitarbeiter und einem Kunden ein klares und eindeutiges Bild der CA stehen: das einer dynamischen, weltoffenen Grossbank mit internationalem Charakter.

Au cours des années soixante et soixante-dix, la structure économique a connu un changement plus profond que jamais auparavant. En raison du nombre croissant de succursales et des aspects toujours plus diversifiés de la communication écrite, la CA a connu les formes de présentation les plus variées. Du point de vue du département concerné, chacune de ces solutions avait son utilité et sa raison d'être, mais le «non initié» éprouvait nécessairement quelque peine à reconnaître *sa* CA derrière cette multiplicité d'aspects divers.

Des institutions telles que la CA ont besoin d'éléments bien déterminés pour exprimer avec conviction les caractéristiques spécifiques à leur personnalité; car l'image que le public se fait de la CA – son renom et sa notoriété – dépend essentiellement de la qualité de l'identité visuelle. C'est à partir d'elle que l'on jugera de la compétence, voire même de l'importance économique de la banque. Chaque prise de contact entre l'un de nos collaborateurs et un client doit être étayée par une image claire et bien définie de la CA: celle d'une grande banque dynamique, ouverte sur le monde et aux activités internationales.

En partant de l'image ainsi conçue et largement diffusée de la CA, le profil CA clairement reconnaissable doit permettre d'établir une association d'idées spontanée avec la qualité de nos performances. La continuité que nous cherchons à réaliser dans nos présentations doit affirmer notre identité, renforcer notre personnalité et susciter l'adhésion positive à notre banque. Cette continuité ne s'applique

CREDITANSTALT

Building upon the aforementioned and known picture of the CA, the clearly recognizable CA image must spontaneously create an association with our performance. The aspired continuity of appearances should produce identity, personality and the desired positive response. This aspired continuity does ideally not only include advertising, catalogues and in-house printed matters; just as important are: The architecture of the buildings, designing and equipping branch offices, marking of company vehicles, dressing and in particular demeanour of employees as well as the written language of all correspondence.

A systematized logo, a combination of symbol and script are fundamental for a uniform appearance. The CA sign as such will not be changed (identification!). Just the appearance of the sign was clearly defined: The "CA" is white in a red square. All other forms, as a free-standing CA, negative showings (red CA in white square), other colors, etc., were skipped after thorough investigation.
The logo may appear in black or grey only on black-and-white printed matters. The symbol must always appear as a logo together with the lettering (for foreign countries and in addresses one or more sub-lines may be added).
The design of the logo is based on the "one fifth system", which was also used in all other design principles. The lettering, for instance, is ⅖th of the symbol height and is ⅗th of the symbol height removed from the symbol. The printer's screens have also been subdivided into 5 columns.

Aufbauend auf dem für die CA vorangegangenen und bekannten Bild, soll das eindeutig wiedererkennbare CA-Profil spontan die Assoziation zu unserer Leistungsfähigkeit herstellen. Die angestrebte Beständigkeit in den Auftritten soll uns Identität, Persönlichkeit und die gewünschte positive Zuwendung bringen. Zu dieser angestrebten Beständigkeit zählt im Idealfall nicht nur die Gestaltung der Werbung, Prospekte und Hausdrucksachen, ebenso wichtig sind: Architektur der Gebäude, Ausgestaltung der Filialen, Kennzeichnung der Firmenwagen, Bekleidung und besonders das Auftreten der Angestellten sowie der Umgangston im Schriftverkehr.

Grundstein des Erscheinungsbildes ist das systematisierte Logo, eine Zeichen-Schriftzug-Kombination. Das CA-Zeichen bleibt dabei unverändert (Identifikation!). Es wurde nur eine konstante Abbildungsweise festgelegt: Das «CA» steht weiss in dem roten Quadrat. Alle anderen Formen, wie freistehendes CA, negatives Zeichen (rotes CA vor weissem Quadrat), andere Farben usw., wurden nach eingehender Prüfung ausgeschieden. Nur bei Schwarzweissdruck darf das Zeichen in Schwarz oder Grau abgebildet werden. Das Zeichen soll immer nur als Logo, zusammen mit dem Schriftzug, dargestellt sein (für das Ausland und Adressenangaben können noch eine oder mehrere Unterzeilen hinzugefügt werden).
Hinter der Gestaltung des Logos steht eine «Fünftel-Systematik», die auch in allen anderen Gestaltungsrichtlinien Verwendung fand. So hat der Schriftzug zum Beispiel ⅖ der Zeichenhöhe und ist ⅗ der Zeichenhöhe vom Zeichen entfernt. Aber auch die Druckraster sind in 5 Spalten aufgeteilt.

pas seulement, dans le cas idéal, à la conception de la publicité, des prospectus et des imprimés de l'entreprise, mais encore à l'architecture des bâtiments, l'aménagement des succursales, les inscriptions sur les voitures d'entreprise, l'habillement et, surtout, la présentation des employés, ainsi que le style et le ton utilisés dans la communication écrite.

La pierre angulaire de l'image d'identification est le logo systématisé, qui est une combinaison entre un symbole et une inscription. Le sigle CA reste inchangé (identification!). Il a simplement été décidé d'utiliser une forme constante de reproduction: le «CA» est en blanc dans un carré rouge. Toutes les autres variantes, telles que le sigle disposé librement, le signe en négatif (CA rouge sur fond blanc), l'utilisation d'autres couleurs, etc. ont été rejetées après examen approfondi.
Seule dans l'impression noir sur blanc, le symbole peut être reproduit en noir ou en gris. Il doit toujours être utilisé uniquement comme logotype, donc en combinaison avec l'inscription (pour l'étranger et l'indication des adresses, il est possible d'ajouter encore une ou plusieurs sous-lignes).
La conception formelle du logotype est fondée sur le principe de la «subdivision en cinquièmes», utilisé également dans d'autres règles de la création graphique. C'est ainsi que l'inscription a une hauteur de ⅖ de la hauteur du symbole et se trouve placée à une distance du symbole égale à ⅗ de la hauteur du signe. Les trames d'impression sont elles aussi subdivisées en 5 colonnes.

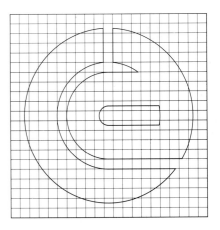

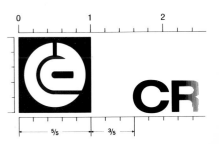

Realization of the New Appearance

Die Realisation des neuen Erscheinungsbildes

La réalisation de la nouvelle image d'identification

The location of the logo co-decides the location of the other elements. The vertical line of the "C" of "Creditanstalt" is the lefthand column edge for picture or text elements above and below. The signet gains in visual significance from the very fact that it alone stands left of this line.

In order to support this "exceptional positioning" of the signet, it must be surrounded by free space as large as its proper dimensions.

If the signet is diminished to less than 1 cm of the page length, the two letters will run into each other and, if diminished even further, will become unrecognizable.

This phenomenon can be optically counterbalanced by widening the distance between the letters.

Durch die Anordnung der Logos wird der Stand der anderen Elemente mitbestimmt. Dabei ist die senkrechte Linie am «C» von «Creditanstalt» der linke Spaltenrand für darüber oder darunter befindliche Bild- oder Textelemente. Das Signet gewinnt dadurch, dass es allein links von dieser Linie steht, an visueller Bedeutung.

Um diese «Ausnahmestellung» des Zeichens zu unterstützen, soll rings um das Zeichen ein Freiraum erhalten bleiben, der der Eigengrösse entspricht.

Wird das Signet auf weniger als 1 cm Seitenlänge verkleinert, dann laufen die beiden Buchstaben zusammen und werden bei weiterer Verkleinerung unkenntlich.

Dieser Erscheinung tritt eine offenere Form entgegen, die durch den vergrösserten Abstand zwischen den Buchstaben eine optischen Ausgleich schafft.

La disposition des logos détermine la position des autres éléments. La ligne verticale du «C» de «Creditanstalt» représente le bord de la colonne gauche pour les éléments d'image ou de texte situés au-dessus ou en dessous. Placé seul à gauche de cette ligne, le sigle gagne ainsi en relief visuel.

Pour souligner cette «position privilégiée» du sigle, il faut garder tout autour un espace libre qui corresponde à la grandeur même du symbole.

Si le sigle est réduit à moins de 1 cm de longueur sur les côtés, les deux lettres se rejoignent et ne sont plus guère identifiable en cas de nouvelle réduction.

Cet inconvénient peut être supprimé grâce à une forme ouverte qui, par un espacement plus grand entre les caractères, crée une compensation optique.

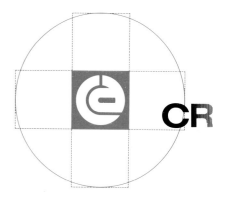

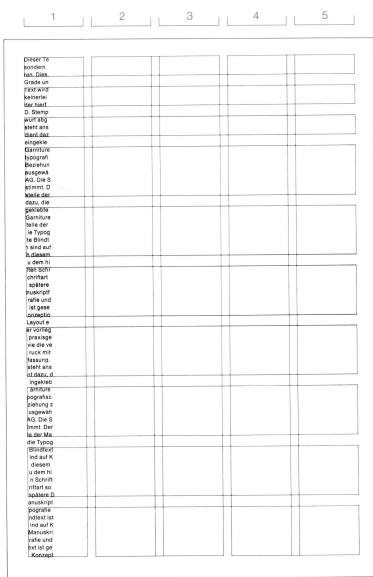

The basic screen for printed matters —
similar to the logo — is based upon
subdividing the DIN A4 sheet into five
sections. The DIN A4 screen then is
decisive for all smaller or larger
screens, which all also have been subdivided into five vertical columns.

Der Grundraster für die Drucksachen
ist – ähnlich wie beim Logo – auf der
fünffachen Aufteilung des DIN-A4-
Blattes aufgebaut. Der DIN-A4-Raster
ist dann «Pate» für alle kleineren oder
grösseren Raster, die auch alle in fünf
senkrechte Spalten aufgeteilt sind.

La trame de base pour les imprimés
se fonde – tout comme pour le logo –
sur la subdivision en cinquièmes de la
feuille DIN A4. La trame DIN A4 est
alors déterminante pour les trames
plus grandes ou plus petites qui sont
toutes subdivisées en cinq colonnes
verticales.

Mini-Gourmet-Lexikon
Weil der Urlaub auch durch den Magen geht.

CREDITANSTALT

Ausgabe 1982

Wissenswertes über Auslandsreisen

CREDITANSTALT

Einfacher geht es nicht

CA-Privat-Sofort-Kredit

CREDITANSTALT

Bequem zu hohem Ertrag. Mit CA-Wertpapieren.

CA-Wertpapier-Konto

CREDITANSTALT

Die CA-Initiative für Leute von 14–19

CA-Konto der Jugend

CREDITANSTALT

Stand: August 1982

Exportieren

CREDITANSTALT

CA-Studenten-service

Schon bei der CA inskribiert?

CREDITANSTALT

Devisen-kurse

Jänner 1982

CREDITANSTALT

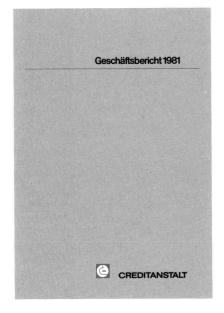

Geschäftsbericht 1981

CREDITANSTALT

I/82

CA-Quarterly

Wirtschaftsinformationen aus Österreich

CREDITANSTALT

CREDITANSTALT

Money-Shop-Courier

Trends:

Junge Leute entdecken die CA

Der Hit der Saison:

Heiße Konten

Übrigens . . .

Neue Strömungen in der Nationalökonomie

Eine Übersicht von Erich Streissler

CREDITANSTALT

Script and Typographical Design of CA Printed Matters

Schrift- und Satzbild der CA-Drucksorten

Les caractères et la conception typographique des imprimés CA

The script is of major importance for an immediatly recognizable picture. W. Schönert wrote:
"Stop bringing design manipulations into script. Not advertising artists, but readers must be satisfied." Using the Helvetica letter family as our CA script, we have, above all, selected a well readable script.
This script in its various forms is holding up for the widely scattered requirements of all of our printed matters in the most uniform way.

All printed matters for quantity texts are based on 9-point Helvetica light.

The consistent order of all screens can clearly be seen in the overall appearance, which printed matters now convey to the reader.

The most spectacular innovation certainly is the grey background — it stands for association: discrete, serious. The signet can well stand out from this grey without being obtrusively large.

Für ein sofort wiedererkennbares Bild ist die Schriftart von grösster Bedeutung. W. Schönert schrieb: «Es sollte mit allen gestalterischen Manipulationen von Schrift Schluss gemacht werden. Es gilt nicht, Werbekünstler zu befriedigen, sondern Leser.» Mit der Helvetica-Schriftenfamilie als unserer CA-Hausschrift haben wir vor allem eine gut lesbare Schrift gewählt. Diese Schriften sind auch den enorm gefächerten Anforderungen aller unserer Drucksachen am gleichmässigsten gewachsen.

Allen Drucksachen liegt für den Mengentext die 9 Punkt Helvetica mager zugrunde.

Die durchgehende Ordnung in allen Rastern zeigt sich deutlich in dem aufgeräumten Gesamtbild, das die Drucksachen dem Leser jetzt bieten.

Die auffälligste Neuerung ist sicher der graue Fond – er steht für die Assoziation: diskret, seriös. Das Signet kann sich von diesem Grauton hervorragend abheben, ohne aufdringlich gross sein zu müssen.

Pour qu'une conception soit spontanément identifiable, le type des caractères utilisés est d'importance capitale. W. Schönert a écrit: «Il faudrait mettre un terme à toute manipulation graphique de la typographie. Il s'agit de satisfaire non pas l'artiste publicitaire, mais le client.» Avec le choix de la famille de caractères Helvetica pour la CA, nous disposons de caractères facilement identifiables, qui répondent aux exigences fort variées de nos imprimés.

Tous nos imprimés ont pour base l'Helvetica maigre de 9 points pour la composition des textes courants.

L'ordre systématique inhérent à toutes les trames s'exprime clairement à travers l'image globale de bonne facture que les imprimés offrent désormais au lecteur.

L'innovation la plus frappante est incontestablement le fond gris qui évoque les qualités d'une entreprise «discrète» et «sérieuse». Le sigle ressort fort bien sur ce fond gris, sans s'imposer par sa grandeur excessive.

Konzernkonferenz der Creditanstalt
19. November 1981

Klaus Barthelt
Ist die Energieversorgung nach 1985 gesichert?

Ernst Fiala
Technische Innovation als Motor des Wirtschaftswachstums

CREDITANSTALT

I/82

CA Quarterly

Facts and Figures
on Austria's Economy

CREDITANSTALT
Vienna/Austria

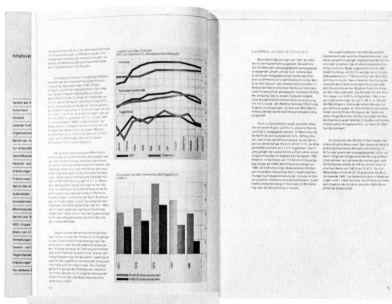

CREDITANSTALT
Buchungsbeleg

CREDITANSTALT

edv-service

CREDITANSTALT

Beteiligungsfonds-gesetz

Eine systematische Darstellung
von Walther Kastner und Herbert Kotrnoch

CREDITANSTALT

Wer bar bezahlt, kauft günstiger.
Nützen Sie jetzt diesen Vorteil durch den

CA-Privat-Sofort-Kredit

CREDITANSTALT

CA's Appearance in Public

Das Auftreten der CA in der Öffentlichkeit

La présentation de la CA en public

Our identity depends on the creation of a mutual tone and mutual expression; and not just on a definitive external effect. Our public must not be approached in a soberly informative manner on one occasion, and obtrusively the next time. We could lose effect and credibility — or both — should we attempt to appear as a faceless, chameleon-like enterprise. Taking into consideration the taming of all creative richdoms of ideas on the basis of our graphic guidelines, we graphic specialists still have enough freedom to sensibly handle all design tasks. The typical CA typography will always give printed materials their unique appearance.

Wichtig für unsere Identität ist die Schaffung eines gemeinsamen Tones und einer gemeinsamen Aussage; nicht nur eine feststehende äusserliche Anmutung. Unser Publikum soll nicht einmal nüchtern-informativ und ein andermal marktschreierisch-aufdringlich angesprochen werden. Als ein solch gesichtsloses, chamäleonhaft sich wandelndes Unternehmen hätten wir an Wirkung oder Glaubwürdigkeit verloren – oder an beidem. Bei aller Zähmung des kreativen Ideenreichtums durch unsere grafischen Richtlinien bleiben den Grafikern noch genug Freiheiten zur zweckmässigen Umsetzung aller Gestaltungsaufgaben. Das CA-typische Satzbild drückt den Drucksachen immer seinen unverkennbaren Stempel auf.

La création d'un «ton» commun et d'une manière commune de s'exprimer est essentielle pour l'identité de la CA. Il faut éviter de s'adresser au public tantôt sous forme d'informations objectives, tantôt à grands cris et avec agressivité. Si nous réagissions à la manière d'un caméléon ou d'une entreprise «sans visage», nous perdrions (littéralement!) la face ou notre fiabilité, voire même les deux. Bien que la profusion d'idées créatives soit quelque peu endiguée par nos lignes directrices sur la création graphique, les graphistes disposent encore de suffisamment de libertés pour leurs réalisations. La conception typographique caractéristique de la CA imprime très clairement son sceau à tous les imprimés de l'entreprise.

Mehr persönliche Finanzkraft durch eine gute Bankverbindung.

Mehr persönliche Finanzkraft durch eine gute Bankverbindung.

Mehr persönliche Finanzkraft durch eine gute Bankverbindung.

Mehr persönliche Finanzkraft durch eine gute Bankverbindung.

CREDITANSTALT

Mehr persönliche Finanzkraft durch eine gute Bankverbindung.

CREDITANSTALT

Mehr persönliche Finanzkraft durch eine gute Bankverbindung.

CREDITANSTALT

Expression:
The ''Handwriting''
of the CA

Die Ausdrucksweise:
«Handschrift» der CA

La manière
de s'exprimer:
l'«écriture» de la CA

Past the design, the customer also senses the personally meant undertone, which is present in all external messages. Whenever and however the customer or business partner is approached—it should always be done seriously, but also in a personal, natural tone of voice.

Über das Design hinaus spürt der Kunde auch den gefühlsmässigen Unterton, der in allen Aussagen enthalten ist. Bei welcher Gelegenheit der Kunde bzw. Geschäftspartner auch angesprochen wird – immer sollte dies in zwar seriösem, gleichzeitig aber auch persönlichem, unverkrampftem Ton geschehen.

Par-delà le design, le client perçoit le ton sous-jacent subjectif, implicitement contenu dans tout message de l'entreprise.
Chaque fois que la banque s'adresse aux clients ou à ses partenaires d'affaires, elle doit trouver le ton juste, un ton à la fois sérieux, personnel et décontracté.

The letterheads were made up following the directions of the Austrian Standards Institute. The available space has been used rationally and economically.
The address space of the letterhead is somewhat smaller than the window area of the envelope. This prevents a possible sliding away of portions of the address.
The uniform subdivision of the forms also creates the prerequisites for economical handling.

Die Briefbogen wurden nach den Richtlinien des österreichischen Normungsinstituts entworfen und gewährleisten eine rationelle und ökonomische Raumnutzung.
Das Adressenfeld der Briefbogen ist etwas kleiner als das Sichtfenster der Umschläge. So wird ein eventuelles Abrutschen von Teilen der Adresse aus dem Sichtfeld verhindert.
Auch die gleichbleibende Einteilung der Formulare schafft die nötigen Voraussetzungen für eine wirtschaftliche Betriebsführung.

Les en-têtes de lettres ont été conçues conformément aux directives de l'Institut autrichien de normalisation et assurent une utilisation rationnelle et économique de la place disponible.
L'espace réservé à l'adresse est légèrement plus petit que la fenêtre de l'enveloppe. Il est ainsi possible d'éviter que certaines parties de l'adresse ne soient plus visibles à cause du glissement de la feuille à l'intérieur de l'enveloppe.
La subdivision, toujours identique, des formulaires crée les conditions nécessaires à une gestion rationnelle.

Further Development of the Existing

Die Weiterentwicklung des Bestehenden

Le constant perfectionnement de ce qui existe

Towards the end of 1982 there was a plan and concept for the new Corporate Identity of the CA; a Design Manual was put together, starting from the branch office through advertising for Railway, Bus and Public all the way to the smallest detail as door signs and letter boxes.
To us, this Manual is not the finalization of Corporate Identity; it is rather just an aid towards final implementation.

Ende 1982 war die Planung und Konzeption für die neue CI der CA beendet, und es wurde ein Design-Manual zusammengestellt, angefangen mit der Gestaltung der Filialen über die Werbung an Bahn, Bus und Bande bis zu den kleinsten Details, wie Türschildchen oder den Briefkästen. Dieses Manual ist für uns nicht der Abschluss der CI; vielmehr ist es nur ein Hilfsmittel bei der endgültigen Realisation.

Fin 1982, la planification et la conception de la nouvelle CI de la CA étaient terminées, et un manuel de design a été réalisé sur la conception formelle des succursales, la publicité dans les gares et les moyens de transport publics, jusqu'aux menus détails, tels que les écriteaux sur les portes ou les inscriptions sur les boîtes à lettres. Pour nous, ce manuel ne marque pas l'achèvement de la CI; il constitue simplement un instrument contribuant à la réalisation finale.

⊕ ISOLE**EOLIE**

Mimmo Castellano

An incidential project
Project No. 1

Ein zufällig entstandenes Projekt
Projekt Nr. 1

Un projet né du simple hasard
Projet n° 1

ALBERGHI OSTELLI E CAMPING	RISTORANTI	ARCHEOLOGIA	UFFICI	ARRIVI E PARTENZE
1 Carasco Hotel	16 Al Pirata	A Museo Archeologico	25 Municipio	41 Porto e biglietteria Aliscafi
2 Rocce azzurre Hotel	17 Da Pescecane	B Parco Archeologico	26 Azienda Aut. Soggiorno e Turismo	42 Porto e biglietteria navi e traghetti
3 Giardino sul mare Hotel	18 E Pulera	**ARTE**	27 Guardia di Finanza	**OFFICINE**
4 Gattopardo Park Hotel	19 Filippino	C Cattedrale	28 Capitaneria di Porto	43 Officine meccaniche o navali
5 Pensione Villa Diana	20 Galeone	D Chiesa dell'Immacolata	29 Banca del Sud	**RIFORNIMENTI**
6 Augustus Hotel	21 Mistral	E Chiesa dell'Addolorata	30 Banca Agricola Etnea	44 Stazione Esso
7 Europeo Albergo	22 La Pinnata	F Chiesa delle Grazie	31 Ufficio del Registro	45 Stazione Agip
8 Oriente Piccolo Hotel	23 Turmalin	G Chiesa s. Antonio	32 Cassa Centrale di Risparmio V.E.	46 Gasolio agevolato natanti
9 Hotel Regione	**RITROVI**	H Chiesa dei Cappuccini	33 Imposte Dirette e Catasto	**TAXI E RENT A CAR**
10 Pensione Neri	24 Andy Capp Club	**SPORT**	34 Poste e Telegrafi	T Posteggio taxi
11 Locanda del Corso	1 La Meridiana	X Campi da tennis	35 Biblioteca Popolare Comunale	K Nolo vetture
12 Locanda Salina	22 La Pinnata	Y Campo di calcio	36 Pretura	**GIORNALI**
13 Locanda Trinacria	23 Turmalin	Z Campo di pallacanestro e pallavolo	37 Carabinieri	G Quotidiani e riviste
14 Ostello della Gioventù			38 Vigili Urbani	
15 Camping Il Castello			39 Ospedale	
			40 Vescovado	

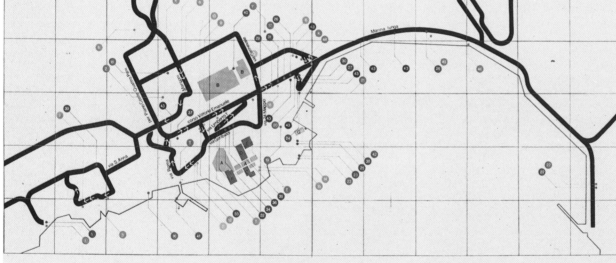

The project does not start with an order.
It comes about, so to speak, by playing around during a holiday trip: Because the author had given up his extensive search for a newspaper and tobacco stand. What comes off it, is a green table investigation, a study of the topography of Lipari, the most significant center of the Lipari Islands. What is concerned is primarily the possibility of communicating tourist news.

Am Anfang des Projekts steht nicht ein Auftraggeber.
Es entsteht sozusagen aus Spielerei während einer Ferienreise: Weil der Autor es aufgegeben hat, lange nach dem Zeitungsverkäufer und dem Tabakladen zu suchen. Was dabei zustande kommt, ist eine vom grünen Tisch aus gemachte Untersuchung, ein Studium der Topografie von Lipari, des wichtigsten Zentrums der Äolischen Inseln. Worum es dabei geht, ist hauptsächlich, die Möglichkeit der Übertragung touristischer Informationen zu ermitteln.

Aucun commettant n'a été à l'origine du présent projet. C'était pour s'amuser, pendant un voyage de vacances, que l'auteur l'a créé, alors qu'il était las de chercher un vendeur de journaux et un magasin de tabac. Ce qui a été ainsi réalisé consiste en une analyse purement théorique, une étude de la topographie de Lipari, le centre le plus important des îles Eoliennes. Il s'agit primairement d'examiner les possibilités de transmettre des informations touristiques.

The Symbol of the Archipelago
First Application of the Symbol
Project No. 2

Das Symbol des Archipels
Erste Anwendung des Symbols
Projekt Nr. 2

Le symbole de l'archipel
Première application du symbole
Projet n° 2

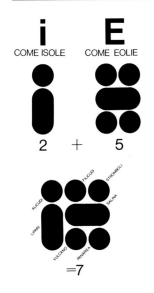

i
COME ISOLE

E
COME EOLIE

2 + 5

=7

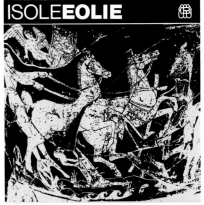

ISOLE**EOLIE**

A further project without anyone who ordered it, entirely borne from improvising, is the draft of the symbol of the group of islands. After several research activities in the historic, mythic, religious and ethnic fields, a numerical/geological solution was given preference.
Numerical/alphabetical, because the seven elements are in conformity with the initials "I" (Isole) and "E" (Eolie), and because seven is the number of the islands.
Geological, because these elements were given a truncated cone periphery, as is typical for islands of volcanic origin.

Ein weiteres Projekt ohne Auftraggeber, gänzlich aus der Improvisation heraus entstanden, ist der Entwurf des Symbols der Inselgruppe. Nach mehreren Forschungen im historischen, mythischen religiösen und ethnischen Bereich wurde einer numerisch-geologischen Lösung der Vorzug gegeben.
Numerisch-alphabetisch, weil die sieben Elemente den Initialen «I» (Isole) und «E» (Eolie) entsprechen und weil sieben die Zahl der Inseln ist.
Geologisch, weil diesen Elementen ein kegelstumpfförmiger Umfang gegeben wurde, wie er für Inseln vulkanischen Ursprungs charakteristisch ist.

Un autre projet sans commettant, né de l'improvisation la plus totale, est le croquis du symbole de tout le groupe d'îles. Après divers travaux de recherche dans les domaines historique, mythique, religieux et éthique, c'est la solution géologique-numérique qui a eu la préférence.
La méthode alpha-numérique a été retenue parce que les sept éléments correspondent aux initiales «I» (Isole) et «E» (Eolie) et que les îles sont au nombre de sept.
L'approche géologique a été choisie parce que ces éléments ont été dotés d'une configuration conique tronquée qui correspond aux formes typiques des îles d'origine volcanique.

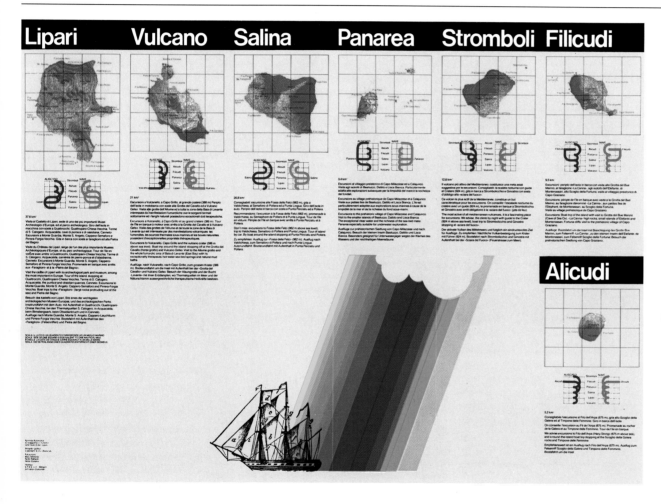

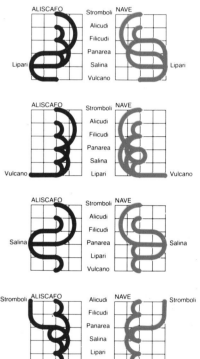

While elaborating the individual items of information, special attention is attributed to explaining the rather complicated ways of reaching the various islands in a series of graphic pictures. Had one put this information into words, they would have been awkward and not very easily understood. Shown graphically, however, they become immediately understandable and legible.

Beim Ausarbeiten der einzelnen Informationen wird besonders darauf geachtet, dass die recht komplizierten Arten, die verschiedenen Inseln zu erreichen, durch eine Reihe von grafischen Darstellungen erklärt werden. Würde man diese Informationen in Worte fassen, wären sie umständlich und daher nicht leicht zu verstehen, in grafische Zeichen umgesetzt, werden sie dagegen unmittelbar verständlich und lesbar.

Dans l'élaboration des différentes informations, il importait d'expliquer par une série de représentations graphiques le mode d'accès souvent fort complexe pour parvenir aux différentes îles. Ces mêmes informations, exprimées en paroles, seraient compliquées et difficiles à saisir, alors que la transposition en signes graphiques leur donne une forme claire et directement accessible.

An Ocean Map
A further
parallel project

Eine Seekarte
Ein weiteres
paralleles Projekt

Une carte maritime
Un autre
projet parallèle

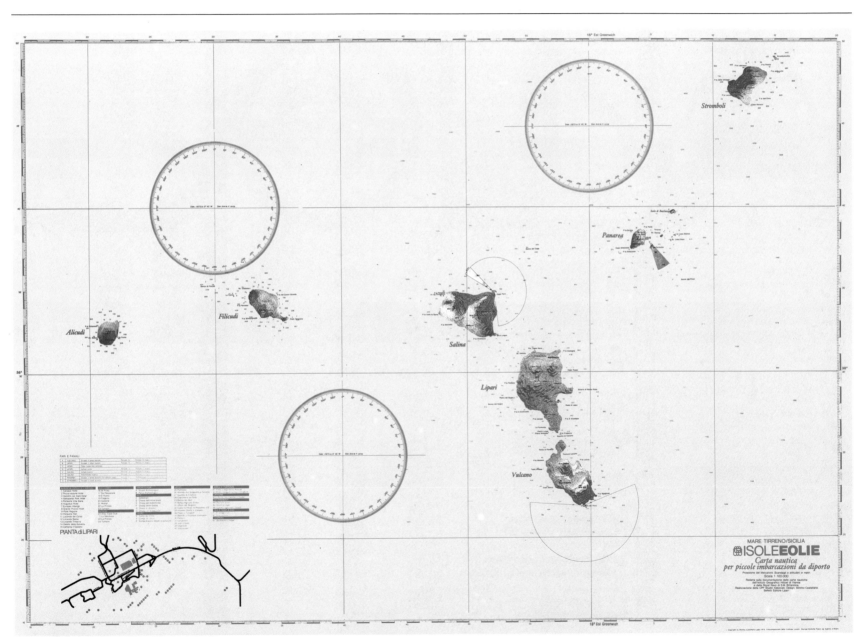

Such a map is necessary, because on official maps the Archipelago is shown torn apart on two maps, with which one cannot navigate.

Eine solche Karte ist deshalb notwendig, weil auf den offiziellen Karten der Archipel in zwei Karten auseinandergerissen dargestellt ist, womit sich nicht navigieren lässt.

Une telle carte s'avère indispensable parce que sur les cartes officielles, l'archipel est coupé en deux et présenté sur deux cartes distinctes, ce qui rend la navigation difficile.

Project of General Tourist Orientation, Project No. 3

Projekt einer allgemeinen Fremdenverkehrssignalisierung Projekt Nr. 3

Projet général d'information touristique Projet n° 3

 Consulates
Konsulate
Consulats

 News agency
Zeitungsagentur
Agence de presse

 Taxi
Taxi
Taxi

 Rent-a-car
Mietwagen
Voiture de location

 Garage
Garage
Garage

 Vehicle breakdown assistance
Autoreparaturhilfe
Service-assistance automobile

 Parking lot
Parkplatz
Parking

 Service station
Wartungsdienst
Station de service

 Petrol station
Tankstelle
Station à essence

 Buses
Busse
Autobus

 Subways
Unterführungen
Passages souterrains

 Bank and exchange
Bank und Wechselstube
Banque et change

 Barber
Herrenfrisör
Coiffeur pour hommes

 Beauty parlour
Damenfrisör
Coiffeur pour dames

 Photographic assistance
Fotohilfe
Assistance photographique

 Photographic equipment
Fotoausstattung
Equipement photographique

 Supermarket
Supermarkt
Supermarché

 Luggage Deposit
Gepäckaufbewahrung
Consigne à bagages

Public Sports Facilities
Öffentliche Sporteinrichtungen
Installations sportives publiques

 Football field
Fussballplatz
Stade de football

 Mini-football field
Minifussballplatz
Mini-stade de football

 Archery
Bogenschiessen
Tir à l'arc

 Marksmanship
Zielschiessen
Tir sur cible

 Clay-pigeon shooting
Tontaubenschiessen
Tir aux plateaux

 Croquet
Crocket
Croquet

 Bowls
Kegeln
Quilles

 Golf
Golf
Golf

 Minigolf
Minigolf
Minigolf

 Volleyball
Volleyball
Volley-ball

 Basketball
Korbball
Basket-ball

 Waterpolo
Wasserpolo
Water-polo

 (Ten-pin) bowling
Bowling
Bowling

 Tennis
Tennis
Tennis

Spare time and entertainment
Freizeit und Unterhaltung
Loisirs et divertissements

 Cinema
Kino
Cinéma

 Theatre
Theater
Théâtre

 Casino
Spielbank
Casino

 Discotheque
Diskothek
Discothèque

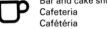 Night Club, whisky à go go
Nachtclub, Whisky à go go
Night Club, Whisky à go go

Bar and cake shop
Cafeteria
Cafétéria

Hotel accommodation
Hotelunterkunft
Hébergement à l'hôtel

Loc with 2nd class hotels or over
Zweitkl. oder bessere Hotels
Hôtels 2e cat. ou cat. supérieure

Loc with 3rd class hotels or under
Drittkl. oder schlechtere Hotels
Hôtels 3e cat. ou cat. inférieure

De luxe hotel
Luxushotel
Hôtel de luxe

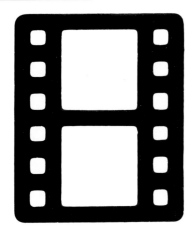

 1st class hotel
Erstklassiges Hotel
Hôtel de 1re catégorie

 2nd class hotel, 1st class boarding house
Zweitklassiges Hotel, erstklassige Pension
Hôtel 2e catégorie, pension 1re catégorie

 3rd class hotel, 2nd class boarding house
Drittklassiges Hotel, zweitklassige Pension
Hôtel 3e catégorie, pension 2e catégorie

 4th class hotel, 3rd class boarding house
Viertklassiges Hotel, drittklassige Pension
Hôtel 4e catégorie, pension 3e catégorie

 Maisonettes, residence
Appartement-Hotel
Maisonnettes, appartements «résidence»

 Bungalows
Bungalows
Bungalows

 Tourist village — hotel and residential
Touristendorf – Hotel und Wohnanlage
Village de-vacances – hôtel et
appartements résidentiels

 Residential tourist village
Dauertouristendorf
Village de tourisme résidentiel

 Tourist village — hotel
Touristendorf – Hotel
Village de vacances – hôtel

 Kinderheim
Kinderheim
Maison d'enfants

Other accommodation
Andere Unterbringung
Autres formes d'hébergement

 Camping ground for caravans and tents
Campingplatz für Wohnwagen und Zelte
Place de camping pour caravanes et tentes

 Caravan campsite
Wohnwagenanlage
Place de caravaning

 Camping ground
Campingplatz
Places de camping

 Youth hostel
Jugendherberge
Auberge de jeunesse

Eating places and wine cellars
Speiselokale und Weinkeller
Etablissements de restauration et caves à vin

Restaurant
Restaurant
Restaurant

Restaurant with garden
Restaurant mit Garten
Restaurant avec jardin

Trattoria
Trattoria
Trattoria

Characteristic restaurant
Spezialitätenrestaurant
Restaurant de spécialités
gastronomiques

15 information groups are defined: nature, culture, off-time, sports, restaurants, hotels, traffic connections, etc. This results in more than 180 pictograms, for which a specific graphic language is developed (see Mimmo Castellano/Graphic and Photographic, Symbols, Trademarks and Logotypes). Color combinations group them into families.

Es werden 15 Informationsgruppen definiert; Natur, Kultur, Freizeit, Sport, Restaurants, Hotels, Verkehrsverbindungen usw. Das Resultat sind über 180 Piktogramme, für die eine eigene grafische Sprache entwickelt wird (siehe Mimmo Castellano/Graphic and Photographic, Symbols, Trademarks and Logotypes). Durch Farbkombinationen werden sie in Familien aufgeteilt.

15 groupes d'information sont définis: la nature, la culture, les loisirs, les sports, les restaurants, les hôtels, les voies de communication, etc. Il en résulte plus de 180 pictogrammes pour lesquels un langage graphique spécifique a été créé (voir Mimmo Castellano/Graphic and Photographic, Symbols, Trademarks and Logotypes). Les combinaisons de couleurs permettent de les subdiviser en familles de pictogrammes.

98055

The Project in the Phase of Implementation

Das Projekt in der Phase der Realisierung

Le projet dans la phase de la réalisation

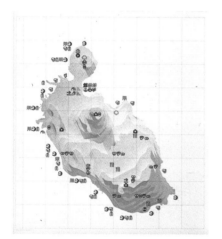

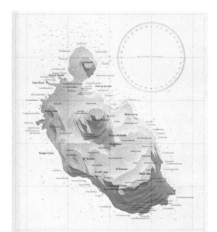

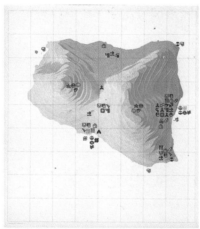

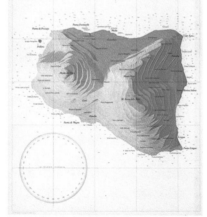

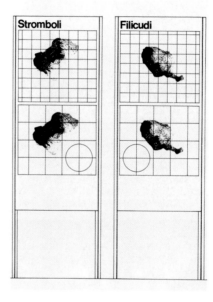

To guide tourists, the various piers of the islands are given orientation signs.
The information system consists of two basic maps: an ocean map, whereby the side of the screen quadrangle corresponds to one sea mile, and an island map, where the screen side corresponds to 1 km.
The most important centers are shown on a topographic map, where the screen side corresponds to 200 m. This book shows the map of the City of Lipari.

Zur Leitung der Touristen sind an den verschiedenen Anlegeplätzen der Inseln eine Reihe von Orientierungsschildern zu schaffen.
Das Informationssystem besteht aus zwei Grundkarten: einer Seekarte mit der Seite des Rasterquadrats entsprechend einer Seemeile und einer Landkarte mit der Rasterseite entsprechend 1 km.
Für die wichtigsten Zentren ist eine topographische Karte mit der Rasterseite entsprechend 200 m vorgesehen. Im vorliegenden Band ist diejenige der Stadt Lipari abgebildet.

Pour guider les touristes, des panneaux d'orientation sont placés aux divers points d'accostage des îles.
Le système d'information se compose de deux cartes de base: une carte maritime, avec la page de trame correspondant à l'échelle de 1 mille marin, et une carte terrestre avec une trame correspondant à l'échelle de 1 km.
Pour les principaux centres, une carte topographique est prévue avec une trame correspondant à 200 m. Dans le présent ouvrage, la carte reproduite est celle de la ville de Lipari.

ZDF

Peter Wittstatt
Design: Otl Aicher

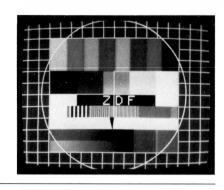

The ZDF – german television, chanel 2 – was founded to give the Federal Republic of Germany a second independent television program. It is a public benefit enterprise of the Public Law — a non-profit enterprise — which is financed by legally stipulated fees and controlled by public organizations. In a representative way these organizations stand for the interests of the politically, ideologically and socially relevant forces by plural vote. For the Corporate Identity of the TV Station ZDF the design of business papers, printed matters, markings and orientation systems are by far less significant than the million-fold multiplied appearances on the screen. By nature, a television program is heterogeneous, not comparable to consumer goods made in series or controllable services. Each contribution is tied down to a certain amount of time, and from its contents and formally, it is unique.

The contents are event-related or characterized by a pre-determined subject. The form of presentation is just as dependent of the contents, as it is of the individual journalistic and artistic self-identification of the individual program manipulators.

Credibility and quality of the information presented by television, however, is increasingly more derived from the degree of familiarity of the publishing enterprise, and less from the author's or interpreter's names.

The Corporate Identity of ZDF lives with and through the permanent conflict between the heterogeneous program interests and from the design plea to make each appearance of the enterprise identifiable through a world of symbols independent of the individual event.

Das Zweite Deutsche Fernsehen – ZDF –wurde gegründet, um in der Bundesrepublik Deutschland ein zweites unabhängiges Fernsehprogramm auszustrahlen. Es ist eine gemeinnützige Anstalt des öffentlichen Rechts – ein «Non-Profit»-Unternehmen –, das durch gesetzlich geregelte Gebührenanteile finanziert und durch Organe kontrolliert ist. In diesen Organen sind in repräsentativer Weise die Interessen der politisch, weltanschaulich und gesellschaftlich relevanten Kräfte pluralistisch vertreten.

Für die Corporate Identity der Fernsehanstalt ZDF ist die Ausformung der Geschäftspapiere, Drucksachen, Objektkennzeichnungen und Orientierungssysteme weit weniger relevant als die millionenfach multiplizierten Erscheinungsauftritte auf dem Bildschirm.

Ein Fernsehprogramm ist naturgemäss heterogen, nicht vergleichbar mit serienmässig gefertigten Konsumgütern oder kontrollierbaren Dienstleistungen. Jeder Beitrag ist zeitgebunden, inhaltlich und formal ein Unikat. Die Inhalte sind ereignisbezogen oder durch ein vorbestimmtes Sujet geprägt. Die Darbietungsform ist vom Inhalt ebenso abhängig wie von der individuellen journalistischen und künstlerischen Profilierung der jeweiligen Programmrealisatoren.

Glaubwürdigkeit und Qualität der im Fernsehen verbreiteten Informationen werden jedoch zunehmend am Bekanntheitsgrad des publizistischen Unternehmens abgeleitet, weniger von den Namen der Autoren oder Interpreten.

Mit und durch den permanenten Konflikt zwischen den heterogenen Programminteressen und dem Design-Anliegen, jeden Erscheinungsauftritt des Unternehmens durch eine vom Einzelereignis unabhängige Zeichen-

La deuxième chaîne de la télévision allemande – ZDF – à été instituée pour permettre la diffusion autonome d'un second programme de télévision en République fédérale d'Allemagne. Il s'agit d'une institution de droit public, à caractère non lucratif; son financement est réglé par des dispositions légales qui lui assurent une quote-part des taxes perçues. Les organes qui contrôlent son activité sont dotés d'une structure pluraliste où sont représentés les intérêts des groupes les plus importants sur le plan politique, idéologique et social.

Pour la Corporate Identity de ZDF, la conception formelle des imprimés d'affaires, des signes distinctifs des produits et des systèmes d'orientation joue un rôle moins déterminant que l'identification de la chaîne à travers les présentations (répétées des millions de fois) sur les écrans de télévision. Un programme de télévision est nécessairement hétérogène. Chaque émission est une contribution unique, du point de vue du fond, de la forme et du temps de diffusion. Son contenu dépend des événements ou est déterminé par un sujet fixé d'avance. Sa forme de présentation est tributaire du fond autant que des aptitudes journalistiques et artistiques des différents réalisateurs.

La fiabilité et la qualité des informations diffusées dépendent toutefois de plus en plus – pour le téléspectateur – de la notoriété de l'entreprise publiciste, et de moins en moins du nom des auteurs ou des interprètes.

La Corporate Identity de la chaîne ZDF vit avec et par le permanent conflit entre les impératifs hétérogènes découlant des programmes et les intérêts spécifiques de la conception formelle, dont le but est de rendre chaque présentation de l'entreprise identifiable grâce à un monde de sym-

In the early seventies Otl Aicher's office for visual communication was endowed with the design of a visual appearance based on standards and systematic design conventions. The diversity of the programs, persons and opinions, which make ZDF as an institution, should find their expression in a uniform form of presentation. Aicher's draft avoids artificial product decoration and company heraldics. He concentrates on relatively simple, natural appearing visual characteristics. The accoustical side of the medium remains a matter of individual preferences in this process. This approach is aimed at very few constant factors only, and a multitude of variables, whose significance will only show in a versatile application. The graphic elements are reduced to typeface and a specific color spectrum, studio design based on standard building elements and a uniform furnishing system.

The efficiency, and at the same time the problem of this Corporate Identity does by far less rest upon a formally aesthetic or decorative scenery. It rests upon interest coordination to achieve a consistent and lasting development of uniform design conventions over and against the journalistic and artistic claim for individuality.

welt identifizierbar zu machen, lebt die Corporate Identity des ZDF.

Anfang der siebziger Jahre wurde das Büro für visuelle Kommunikation von Otl Aicher mit dem Entwurf eines auf Normen und systematischen Gestaltungskonventionen beruhenden visuellen Erscheinungsbildes betraut. Die Mannigfaltigkeit der Sendungen, Personen und Meinungen, die das ZDF als Institution ausmachen, sollten in einer durchgängigen Präsentationsform ihre Entsprechung finden. Der Aichersche Entwurf vermeidet artifizielle Produktdekoration und Firmenheraldik, er konzentriert sich auf relativ simple, selbstverständlich anmutende visuelle Merkmale. Die akustische Komponente des Mediums bleibt dabei einer individuellen Gestaltung überlassen. Der eingeschlagene Weg zielt auf ein System mit nur wenigen Konstanten, dafür um so mehr Varianten, deren Signifikanz sich erst aus einer vielseitigen Anwendung ergibt. Die grafischen Elemente reduzieren sich auf Schrift und ein spezifisches Farbspektrum, die Studiolandschaft auf genormte Bauteile und ein einheitliches Möblierungssystem.

Die Effizienz, gleichzeitig die Problematik dieser Corporate Identity, liegt weit weniger an einer formalästhetischen oder dekorativen Ausstattung. Sie liegt in der Interessenkoordination für eine konsequente und durchgängige Durchsetzung einheitlicher Gestaltungskonventionen gegenüber dem journalistischen und künstlerischen Anspruch auf Eigenständigkeit.

boles indépendants de l'événement individuel.

Au début des années soixante-dix, le Bureau de communication visuelle d'Otl Aicher a été chargé d'élaborer un projet pour une image d'identification visuelle, fondée sur les normes et les conventions systématiques régissant la conception formelle. La multiplicité des émissions, des personnes et des opinions que représente la chaîne ZDF en tant qu'institution devait trouver son expression dans une forme de présentation intégrée et harmonieuse. Le projet d'Aicher renonce à toute décoration artificielle des produits et à toute présentation héraldique de l'entreprise, pour se concentrer sur des symboles visuels de caractère évident et de forme relativement simple. La composante acoustique du média reste réservée à la conception individuelle. Les éléments graphiques se réduisent aux caractères typographiques et à une gamme de couleurs spécifiques. Les décors du studio se limitent à des éléments de construction normalisés et à un système d'ameublement uniforme. L'efficience et, simultanément, le caractère problématique de cette Corporate Identity ne réside pas primairement dans sa conception esthétique formelle ou ses qualités décoratives. Elle consiste plutôt dans la coordination des intérêts, dans le but d'assurer l'application conséquente et cohérente des conventions harmonisées sur la conception visuelle face aux besoins d'autonomie qui découlent des exigences artistiques et journalistiques.

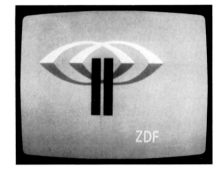

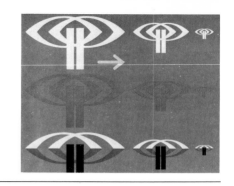

The signet (TV station symbol) goes back to a draft by W. Hörnig. In its application, the momentum of this symbol has been strongly reduced. It is restricted to a more official, representative function, as for instance to documents or official seals. The reason for this decision is the lack of a common-language interpretation of the formation of the signet.

The common abbreviation ZDF for «Zweites Deutsches Fernsehen» is the basis of the development of a Logo. As soon as this letter combination in the relevant ZDF typeface is placed at exactly defined distances, it creates the character of a symbol. This logo is meant to be used on the screen in many variables. It changes in size, ductus and color. This turns the supreme claim usually attributed to every company logo, into something playful. At remaining significance, the attention value can be increased, and it is an indication of the diversity of the television programs.

Das Signet (Senderkennzeichen) geht auf einen Entwurf von W. Hörnig zurück. In der Anwendung ist die Gewichtigkeit dieses Zeichens stark zurückgenommen. Es bleibt einer mehr offiziellen, repräsentativen Funktion, zum Beispiel bei Urkunden oder Dienstsiegeln, vorbehalten. Grund für diese Entscheidung ist das Fehlen einer umgangssprachlichen Entsprechung für die Ausbildung des Bildzeichens.

Aus dem Sprachgebrauch ZDF statt «Zweites Deutsches Fernsehen» entwickelt sich ein Logo. Sobald diese Buchstabenkombination aus der für das ZDF signifikanten Schrift in exakt definierten Abständen gesetzt wird, erhält sie Zeichencharakter. Dieses Logogramm soll auf dem Bildschirm in vielfältigen Varianten verwendet werden. Es wechselt in Grösse, Duktus und Farbe. Damit wird der hoheitliche Anspruch, der üblicherweise jedem Firmenzeichen anhaftet, ins Spielerische abgewandelt. Bei bleibender Signifikanz kann der Aufmerksamkeitswert gesteigert werden, die Vielfalt eines Fernsehprogramms findet ihre Entsprechung.

L'usage du sigle ZDF dans le langage courant, au lieu de la désignation «Zweites Deutsches Fernsehen», a abouti au développement d'un logo. Dès que cette combinaison de lettres est composée avec les caractères typiques pour la chaîne ZDF et avec les espacements exactement définis, elle acquiert valeur de symbole. Le logogramme doit trouver application sur l'écran en de multiples variantes. Il change de dimensions, de forme et de couleur. Ainsi la prétention à une valeur absolue, si typique pour tant de symboles d'entreprise, se transforme et prend un caractère ludique. A signification égale, le degré d'attention peut être renforcé, la variété du programme de télévision trouve une forme d'expression harmonieuse.

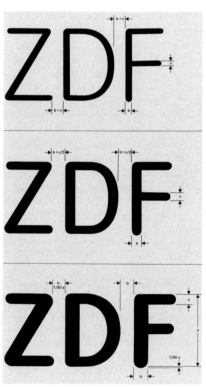

a b c

The typeface in the ZDF Corporate Identity is meant to be a functional carrier of information chosen according to the point of view of fastest possible comprehension. Preliminary tests showed that the Univers typeface designed by Adrian Frutiger best met these conditions. Moreover, these tests showed that the sharp-edged nature of this typeface is lost on the screen, in particular when used in smaller sizes. Thus the Univers typeface was changed into a rounded one, which is typical of ZDF. This is now used to key-line printed materials, which are otherwise printed in Univers 55, and always on the screen. The ductus from light to semi-bold in combination with the colors and all thinkable improvisations stand for the principle of uniformity within diversity.

In der Corporate Identity des ZDF soll die Schrift funktionaler Informationsträger sein, ausgewählt nach den Gesichtspunkten der schnellstmöglichen Erfassbarkeit. Vorversuche ergaben, dass die von Adrian Frutiger gestaltete Univers diese Bedingungen am besten erfüllt. Bei diesen Versuchen ergab sich darüber hinaus, dass der scharfkantige Charakter der Schrift insbesondere bei kleineren Abgrössen auf dem Bildschirm verlorengeht. Damit entwickelte sich aus der Univers die für das ZDF typische Rundschrift. Sie findet ihre Anwendung als Auszeichnung bei Drucksachen, die im übrigen aus der Univers 55 gesetzt werden, und grundsätzlich auf dem Bildschirm. Der Duktus von mager bis schmalfett ergibt in Verbindung mit den Farben und allen denkbaren Verfremdungsarten das Prinzip der Einheitlichkeit in der Vielfalt.

Dans la Corporate Identity de la chaîne ZDF, les caractères typographiques jouent le rôle de supports d'information fonctionnels, sélectionnés en fonction des critères de lisibilité aisée et spontanée. Des études préliminaires ont révélé que les caractères Univers, développés par Adrian Frutiger, répondent le mieux à ces critères. Ces mêmes études ont montré que les bords bien nets des caractères s'estompaient sur l'écran pour les petites forces de corps. C'est cette constatation qui a finalement amené à développer, à partir de l'Univers, la «Ronde» si typique pour ZDF. Ces caractères sont utilisés pour les imprimés, dont le texte est d'ailleurs composé à partir de l'Univers 55, ainsi que pour les réalisations sur l'écran. La forme d'écriture, allant des caractères maigres aux mi-gras étroits, en combinaison avec les couleurs et toutes sortes d'aliénations possibles, permet finalement de retrouver le principe de l'unité dans la multiplicité.

heute journal

DER GROSSE PREIS

Spaß mit Musik

das aktuelle sport-studio

auslands journal

Der Sportspiegel

Bonner Perspektiven

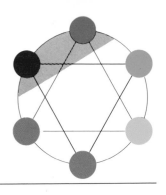

ZDF has no real house color. Even though, a very special blue is given preference; it can be found on letterheads, and also on vehicle labels. On the screen it is often used during news presentations. This blue which originates from electronic color production, however, only is the starting point of a spectrum. A spectrum which gains its significance by the fact that red and violet—colors, which are emotionally attributed to the authoritative sphere, are excluded.

Das ZDF hat keine eigentliche Hausfarbe. Zwar wird einem ganz speziellen blauen Farbton eine Präferenz eingeräumt, er findet sich auf den Briefbogen wie auch in der Kfz-Beschriftung. Auf dem Bildschirm findet er in der Nachrichtenpräsentation eine vermehrte Anwendung. Dieses Blau, das seinen Ursprung in der elektronischen Farberzeugung hat, ist aber lediglich Ausgangspunkt für ein Spektrum. Ein Spektrum, das seine Signifikanz schon dadurch erhält, dass Rot und

La chaîne ZDF n'a pas de «couleur maison» spécifique. Il est vrai que la préférence est donnée à un ton bleu très spécial, utilisé tant pour le papier à lettres que pour les inscriptions sur les véhicules à moteur. Sur l'écran, il trouve de plus en plus fréquemment application. Ce bleu, qui doit son origine à la production électronique des couleurs, est primairement le point de départ d'une gamme de tonalités. Cette gamme acquiert une signification particulière par l'absence du

Thus the color scheme reaches from blue to the complimentary orange, which, in the above meaning as a secondary color, has a signalling function All other colors are a result of defined mixtures. In this system the nature of diversity is reflected. A color fan was developed, from which this attention can be interpreted.

Violett, Farben, die emotional dem autoritären Bereich zugeordnet werden, ausgeklammert sind. Damit reicht der Farbkreis vom Blau bis zum komplementären Orange, das im obengenannten Sinn als Sekundärfarbe Signalfunktion hat. Alle übrigen Farben ergeben sich aus definierten Mischungen. In diesem System findet das Wesen der Vielseitigkeit seinen Niederschlag. Es wurde ein Farbfächer entwickelt, aus dem diese Absicht ablesbar ist.

rouge et du violet, donc de couleurs qui, sous l'angle émotif, se rattachent au domaine autoritaire. Ainsi le cercle chromatique va du bleu à l'orange complémentaire qui, dans le sens mentionné plus haut, acquiert valeur de signal en tant que couleur secondaire. Toutes les autres tonalités se dégagent de mélanges définis. Ce système traduit fort bien l'essence même de la multiplicité. L'éventail des couleurs, développé selon ce principe, révèle clairement cette intention.

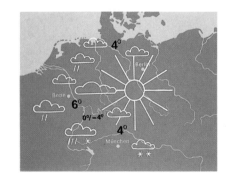

A further opportunity to demonstrate uniformity in diversity results from the obligation to show geographical circumstances in the most various programs. Defined in form and color, maps are an integral part of the visual characteristics of ZDF.

Eine weitere Gelegenheit, Einheitlichkeit in der Vielfalt darzustellen, ergibt sich aus dem Zwang, in den unterschiedlichsten Sendungen geografische Verhältnisse abbilden zu müssen. In Form und Farbe definiert, sind Landkarten ein fester Bestandteil der visuellen Merkmale des ZDF.

Une autre occasion d'exprimer l'unité dans la multiplicité est fournie par l'obligation de reproduire différentes situations géographiques dans les émissions les plus variées. Les cartes géographiques ainsi définies dans leur forme et leurs couleurs deviennent un élément constitutif fixe des caractéristiques visuelles de ZDF.

Sendeschluß

A constant factor of high attention value within television programs is mentioning the time of the day. This finds its visual expression in the TV clock. The fingers and the minute scale have formally been adapted to the typeface of the company. The comprehension of the hour is additionally facilitated by numbers. This conventional, but better legible version of a clock face has preference over just formally explainable or just aesthetic versions.

Eine Konstante von hohem Aufmerksamkeitswert innerhalb eines Fernsehprogramms ist die Zeitangabe, sie findet in der Sendeuhr ihre visuelle Entsprechung. Die Zeiger und die Minuteneinteilung sind formal der Hausschrift angeglichen. Die Erfassbarkeit der Uhrzeit wird durch zusätzlich angebrachte Zahlen gesteigert. Diese konventionelle, aber besser ablesbare Version eines Ziffernblattes hat gegenüber nur formal begründbaren oder nur ästhetischen den Vorzug.

Une constante qui recueille un haut degré d'attention dans le cadre d'un programme de télévision est l'indication de l'heure exacte. Son expression visuelle est le cadran d'une horloge dont les aiguilles et la subdivision en minutes sont formellement adaptées à l'écriture typique de ZDF. Des chiffres viennent encore renforcer la bonne lisibilité de l'heure exacte. Cette conception à la fois conventionnelle et plus aisément déchiffrable du cadran, a reçu la préférence par rapport à d'autres versions purement formelles ou esthétiques.

In order to make Corporate Identity consistent, it is necessary to impose the same requirements on image elements that make the studio scenery, as on graphic image elements. An assortment of high-quality chairs and tables was selected. A variable system of tube supports has the function of tripods, upon which information elements are placed.

The variation spread of this system — especially adapted to the requirements of a television studio, were developed by the Planning Association of H. Kirchhoff.

Für die Durchgängigkeit der Corporate Identity ergibt sich die Notwendigkeit, auch an die Bildelemente, aus denen sich die Studiolandschaft ergibt, ähnliche Anforderungen zu stellen wie an grafische Bildelemente. Ein Sortiment formal hochwertiger Stühle und Tische wurde ausgewählt. Ein variables System von Rohrgestellen hat die Funktion von Stativen, auf denen Informationselemente aufgebracht werden.

Die Variationsbreite dieses Systems – speziell auf die Anforderungen eines Fernsehstudios ausgerichtet – wurde von der Planungsgemeinschaft H. Kirchhoff entwickelt.

Une Corporate Identity intégrée et harmonieuse implique que les éléments d'images qui composent les décors du studio répondent à des exigences aussi élevées que celles que doivent remplir les éléments d'une image graphique. Un assortiment complet de sièges et de tables de haute qualité formelle a été choisi. Un système variable d'échafaudages tubulaires remplit la fonction de supports sur lesquels sont montés les différents éléments d'information.

Ce système aux nombreuses variantes a été développé par la communauté de planification H. Kirchhoff.

Identity Characteristics on the Screen

Identitätsmerkmale auf dem Bildschirm

Les traits caractéristiques de l'image d'identification sur l'écran

Announcements — spoken, written, illustrative program forecasts are not just a table of contents for the daily television program. Constant form elements in their presentation are decisive for identifying the company. Because of the lack of German Federal Republic program magazines in Eastern Germany, these announcements are of special significance for ZDF.

Ansagen – Programmhinweise – sind nicht nur blosses Inhaltsverzeichnis des täglichen Fernsehprogramms. Konstante Formelemente in der Darbietung sind ausschlaggebend für die Identifizierbarkeit des Unternehmens. Beim ZDF bekommen diese Ankündigungen wegen des Fehlens bundesrepublikanischer Programmzeitschriften in der DDR eine besondere Bedeutung.

La présentation du programme de télévision quotidien ne consiste pas en un simple répertoire du contenu. L'utilisation d'éléments constants dans la conception formelle est déterminante pour l'identification de l'entreprise. Le téléprogramme imprimé de la RFA n'étant pas diffusé en Allemagne de l'Est, cet aperçu général du programme de ZDF revêt une importance toute particulière.

The requirement of Corporate Identity to present the mediator of information in a consistent way is of particular importance when it comes to daily news broadcasting.
The make-up is designed and organized in a manner that, whithin a short period of time, i.e. within one half hour news can be visualized individually.

Der Anspruch der CI, den Vermittler von Informationen durchgängig darzustellen, bekommt bei aktuellen Nachrichtensendungen eine besondere Bedeutung.
Die designmässige Ausstattung ist so gestaltet und organisiert, dass kurzfristig innerhalb einer halben Stunde Nachrichteninhalte differenziert visualisiert werden können.

La CI comme symbole d'identification intégré et harmonieux d'un service d'information acquiert un relief particulier dans les émissions d'actualité.
La conception formelle est choisie et organisée de telle manière qu'il devient possible d'assurer à court terme (en l'espace d'une demi-heure) une présentation visuelle différenciée du contenu des informations.

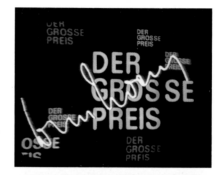

Entertaining programs to quite an extent depend upon decoration, glamour and fashionable effects. It is a continuous challenge for design to use the same elements, which are supposed to represent a company in a "timeless, serious" manner, to put up a show in order to meet with the claim of trivial entertainment for a fashionable and superficial environment.

Unterhaltungssendungen leben nicht zuletzt von Dekor, Glamour und modischen Effekten. Es ist eine fortlaufende Herausforderung an das Design, mit denselben Elementen, die ein Unternehmen «zeitlos, seriös» repräsentieren sollen, vordergründige Show zu machen, um dem Anspruch der Trivialunterhaltung nach einem modischen, auf Äusserlichkeiten beruhenden Ambiente nachzukommen.

Les décors contribuent largement à la fascination des émissions récréatives. C'est un constant défi lancé au «design» que de devoir utiliser les éléments qui confèrent à l'entreprise son caractère «sérieux» pour réaliser une «show» qui réponde à des exigences souvent triviales, un divertissement qui se déroule dans une ambiance fondée sur les apparences et le goût momentané.

Fußball
Bundesliga

Eintr. Bräunschweig	Arminia Bielefeld	3:1
1. FC Kaiserslautern	Borussia M'gladbach	3:2
Borussia Dortmund	VfB Stuttgart	2:3
1. FC Nürnberg	MSV Duisburg	0:0
1. FC Köln	Hamburger SV	1:1
Werder Bremen	SV Darmstadt 98	4:4
Fortuna Düsseldorf	SV 04 Leverkusen	5:1
Eintracht Frankfurt	VfL Bochum	0:1
Karlsruher SC	Bayern München	4:1

Lottozahlen

8 12 26 27 39 45

Zusatzzahl 7

ohne Gewähr

The seriousness of a source of information essentially depends upon its recognition.
The multitude of subjects covered in television, like daily news, culture, entertainment, sciences, sports, requires large variability of the CI constant factors. They have the same significance for recognition of the company as for the representatives on the screen.

Die Seriosität einer Informationsquelle hängt wesentlich von ihrer Identifizierbarkeit ab.
Die thematische Vielfalt eines Fernsehprogramms, Zeitgeschehen, Kultur, Unterhaltung, Wissenschaft, Sport, fordern eine grosse Variabilität der CI-Konstanten; sie haben einen gleichen Stellenwert für die Erkennbarkeit des Unternehmens wie die Präsentatoren auf dem Bildschirm.

Le caractère sérieux d'une source d'information dépend essentiellement de la possibilité de pouvoir l'identifier.
La grande diversité des sujets traités dans un programme de télévision (actualités, culture, divertissement, sciences, sports) exige une grande variabilité des constantes CI. Pour l'identification de l'entreprise, ces constantes ont la même valeur que les présentateurs sur l'écran de télévision.

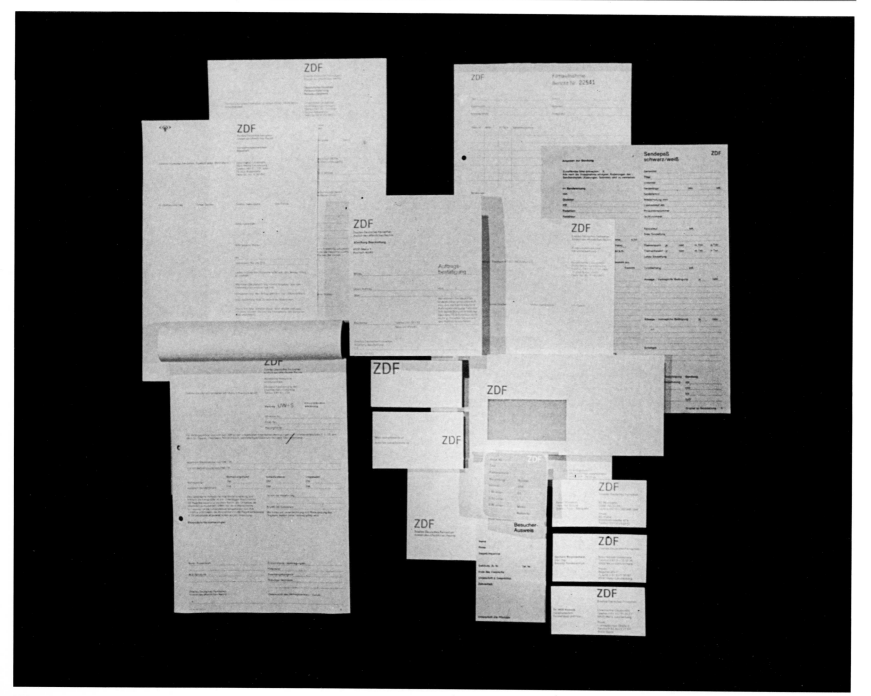

106

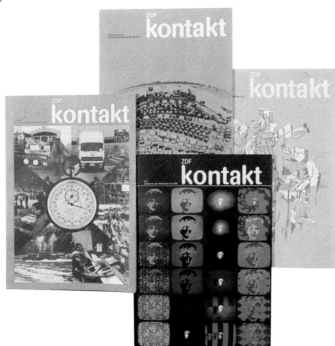

  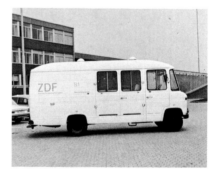 

Printed material of all kind, orientation systems, building identifications down to exhibition halls are also designed according to uniformly developed rules. These rules are described in a two-volume manual.
The effectfulness of all efforts towards company personality, however, does not only rest upon these formally aesthetic conventions; it is governed by every-day, event-related commentaries on the CI rules and central coordination of all pertaining ZDF activities.

Drucksachen, Objektkennzeichnungen bis hin zu Messebauten werden gleichermassen nach durchgängigen Regeln gestaltet. Diese Regeln sind in einem zweibändigen Manual beschrieben.
Die Effizienz aller Bemühungen um die Firmenidentität beruht jedoch nicht allein auf diesen formal-ästhetischen Konventionen, sie wird bestimmt von der ereignisbezogenen Kommentierung der CI-Regeln und der zentralen Koordination aller entsprechenden Aktivitäten beim ZDF.

L'application des caractéristiques CI de ZDF n'est évidemment pas limitée au seul écran de télévision. Elle englobe la conception formelle des imprimés de tout genre, du système d'orientation, des symboles d'identification, jusqu'aux halles d'exposition, selon des règles systématiques. L'efficacité des efforts pour développer l'identité ZDF est largement déterminée par l'interprétation vivante des règles CI à travers les événements quotidiens et par la coordination centrale de toutes les activités ZDF.

MINOLTA

Design:
Saul Bass / Herb Yager & Associates

Minolta
minolta
minolta

Center of Minolta's new corporate identification campaign, the symbol with its precise linear elements conveys the high technology optical and electronic basis of Minolta.
It reflects a company that has moved out of the basically mechanical technology of the past and into the sophisticated world of advanced optics and electronics. The symbol also graphically represents a company that deals with light, and a company that produces high quality products that, in one form or another, process light.

Design Criteria for the Minolta Trademark

General Criteria
The identification should be: unique, memorable, flexible, strong and enduring.

Specific Criteria
Primary:
1 *High Technology:* customers feel that the product is the very latest and most advanced on the market.
2 *Quality:* the product is well made, will last a long time and is reliable.

Secondary:
1 *Vision:* the new identification signals the quality of light, which is the basis of all vision.
2 *Strength:* the company has strong management strength.
3 *Beauty:* the new identification is beautiful, signaling the grace and precision of all Minolta products.
4 *Global:* the new identification will be effective in any country — it transcends language.

Der Mittelpunkt von Minoltas neuer Kampagne zur Unternehmensidentifikation, das Symbol mit seinen klaren linearen Elementen, vermittelt den hohen optischen und elektronischen Stand von Minolta.
Es reflektiert ein Unternehmen, das die mechanische Technologie der Vergangenheit verlassen hat und in die hochentwickelte Welt fortschrittlicher Optik und Elektronik eingedrungen ist. Grafisch stellt das Symbol darüber hinaus ein Unternehmen dar, das sich mit Licht beschäftigt, sowie ein Unternehmen, das qualitativ hochwertige Produkte herstellt, die in der einen oder andern Form Licht verarbeiten.

Gestaltungskriterien für das Warenzeichen Minolta

Allgemeine Kriterien
Die Identität sollte sein: einmalig, wiedererkennbar, flexibel, stark und durchgängig.

Spezifische Kriterien
Primärelemente:
1 *Hochentwickelte Technologie:* der Kunde hat das Gefühl, dass das Produkt das modernste und fortgeschrittenste auf dem Markt ist.
2 *Qualität:* das Produkt ist gut konstruiert, hat eine lange Lebensdauer und ist zuverlässig.

Sekundärelemente:
1 *Erscheinungsform:* die neue Identität strahlt Licht aus, die Basis alles Sichtbaren.
2 *Stärke:* das Unternehmen hat ein starkes Management.
3 *Ästhetik:* die neue Identität ist schön. Sie strahlt die Anmut und Genauigkeit aller Minolta-Produkte aus.
4 *Weltweit:* die neue Identität ist in jedem Land wirkungsvoll.

Point focal de la nouvelle campagne d'identification de l'entreprise Minolta, le symbole aux éléments linéaires rigoureusement définis reflète la haute qualité de la technologie optique et électronique.
Il est l'expression d'une société qui a abandonné la technologie mécanique du passé pour pénétrer dans le monde hautement complexe de l'optique et de l'électronique modernes.
Le symbole est aussi la représentation graphique d'une entreprise qui s'occupe de lumière et qui produit des articles de haute qualité qui, d'une manière ou d'une autre, transforment la lumière.

Critères régissant la conception graphique de la marque Minolta

Critères généraux
L'identification doit être unique, facilement mémorisable, flexible, vigoureuse et durable.

Critères spécifiques
Eléments primaires:
1 *Technologie de pointe:* le client a le sentiment que le produit est le plus moderne et le plus progressiste sur le marché.
2 *Qualité:* le produit est bien conçu, il est durable et fiable.

Eléments secondaires:
1 *Forme de présentation:* la nouvelle identité rayonne et dégage de la lumière, base de tout ce qui est visible.
2 *Force:* l'entreprise est gérée par une direction forte.
3 *Esthétique:* la nouvelle identité est de bonne facture. Elle révèle la conception esthétique et la précision de tous les produits Minolta.
4 *Universalité:* la nouvelle identité agit dans chaque pays, elle «parle» une langue universelle.

110

Symbol/Logo

Logomark

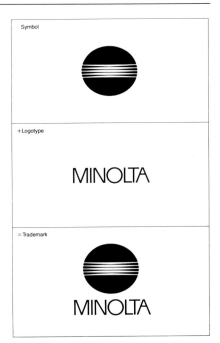

Symbol

+ Logotype

= Trademark

There are two basic configurations of the Minolta trademark, the symbol/ logo and the logomark, which provide for flexibility of use in the wide range of products.

Es gibt zwei grundsätzliche Darstellungen des Markenzeichens Minolta: das Symbol/Logo und das Logozeichen, um bei der Vielzahl von Produkten Flexibilität in der Anwendung zu gewährleisten.

Il existe deux présentations fondamentales de la marque Minolta: le symbole/logo et le logotype pour assurer une grande flexibilité dans l'application sur une vaste gamme de produits.

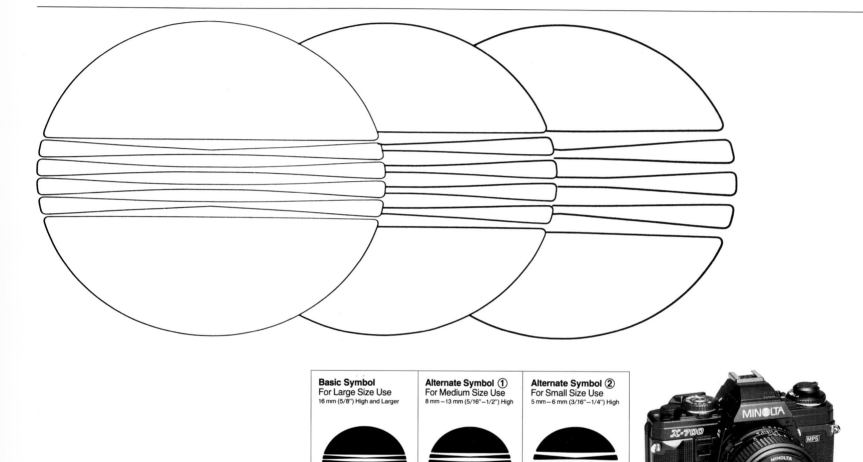

Basic Symbol For Large Size Use 16 mm (5/8″) High and Larger	Alternate Symbol ① For Medium Size Use 8 mm – 13 mm (5/16″–1/2″) High	Alternate Symbol ② For Small Size Use 5 mm – 6 mm (3/16″–1/4″) High

The trademark must work equally well in vertical or horizontal areas, in small and large spaces, and on a wide variety of surfaces.

Das Warenzeichen muss überall gleich funktionieren: in vertikalen und horizontalen Bereichen, im kleinen und im grossen Raum sowie auf einer Vielzahl verschiedener Oberflächen.

La marque doit rester percutante partout: en disposition verticale ou horizontale, dans de petits ou grands espaces et sur une grande diversité de surfaces.

Identification as "marketing tool" on product packages and brochures

Identifizierung als «Marketing-Werkzeug» auf Produktverpackungen und Broschüren

Identification: «instrument de marketing» sur le conditionnement des produits et dans diverses brochures

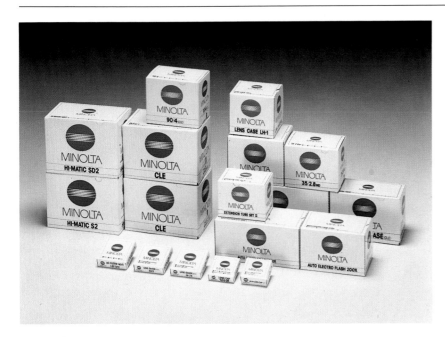

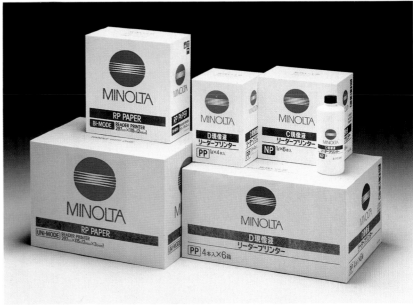

そして 空気は 流れを 忘れた

X-700
MINOLTA PROGRAM SYSTEM

MINOLTA

Minolta: "photography that brings people together"

Little Peter, arms outstretched,
mimicking a scarecrow:
memories of that summertime
to last the years through.

Photography brings people together, and makes the world laugh
and think...and cry. No one knows this better than Minolta,
for we've been mirroring the world, now, for over fifty years.
The Minolta XG-M with Motor Drive 1, Minolta's superb new automatic SLR
that shoots up to 3.5 frames-per-second.

MINOLTA CAMERA CO., LTD., 30, 2-Chome, Azuchi-Machi, Higashi-Ku, Osaka 541, Japan.

Minolta: "photography that brings people together"

Another Saturday, kept indoors.
Gee, Mom: when can we
go outside and play?
Why can't it rain on a school day?

Photography brings people together, and makes the world laugh
and think...and cry. No one knows this better than Minolta,
for we've been mirroring the world, now, for over fifty years.
The Minolta XG-M with Motor Drive 1, Minolta's superb new automatic SLR
that shoots up to 3.5 frames-per-second.

MINOLTA CAMERA CO., LTD., 30, 2-Chome, Azuchi-Machi, Higashi-Ku, Osaka 541, Japan.

Minolta: "photography that brings people together"

Today, the desert is the same as ever:
stark contrasts and colors;
a dignified, proud, nomadic race;
and-above all-the timelessness of the sands.

Photography brings people together, and makes the world laugh
and think...and cry. No one knows this better than Minolta,
for we've been mirroring the world, now, for over fifty years.
The Minolta XG-M with Motor Drive 1, Minolta's superb new automatic SLR
that shoots up to 3.5 frames-per-second.

MINOLTA CAMERA CO., LTD., 30, 2-Chome, Azuchi-Machi, Higashi-Ku, Osaka 541, Japan.

Minolta: "photography that brings people together"

In an Oslo city park,
massive, rock-hewn arms
envelop a playful child,
unmindful of an eternal granite frown.

Photography brings people together, and makes the world laugh
and think...and cry. No one knows this better than Minolta,
for we've been mirroring the world, now, for over fifty years.
The Minolta XG-M with Motor Drive 1, Minolta's superb new automatic SLR
that shoots up to 3.5 frames-per-second.

MINOLTA CAMERA CO., LTD., 30, 2-Chome, Azuchi-Machi, Higashi-Ku, Osaka 541, Japan.

Minolta: "photography that brings people together"

High over the California mountains
your spirits were eagle-high
before your silent sunset landing
to end a perfect day.

Photography brings people together, and makes the world laugh
and think...and cry. No one knows this better than Minolta,
for we've been mirroring the world, now, for over fifty years.
The Minolta XG-M with Motor Drive 1, Minolta's superb new automatic SLR
that shoots up to 3.5 frames-per-second.

MINOLTA CAMERA CO., LTD., 30, 2-Chome, Azuchi-Machi, Higashi-Ku, Osaka 541, Japan.

TV tag sequence
and a TV commercial
with the simplified tag

Fernsehfolge von
Markenzeichen und
Fernsehspot mit
vereinfachtem
Markenzeichen

Séquence TV
et spot télévisé
avec symbole
de marque simplifié

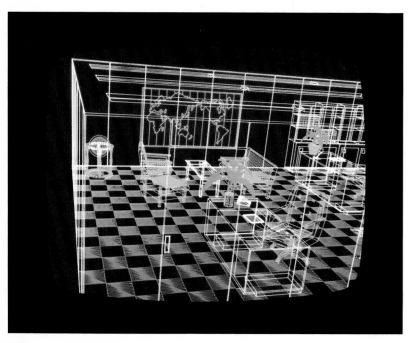

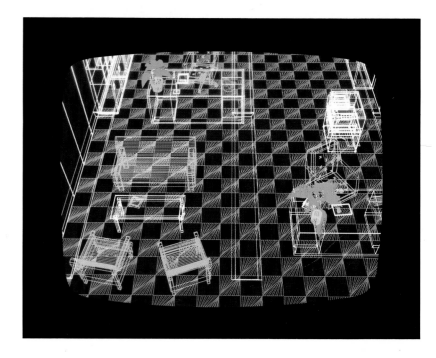

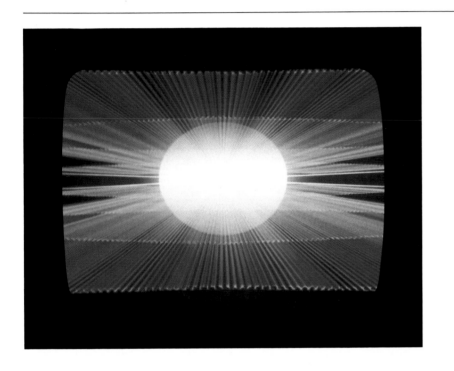

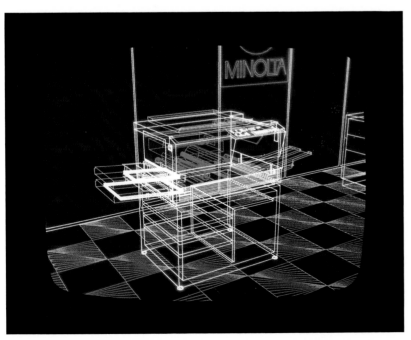

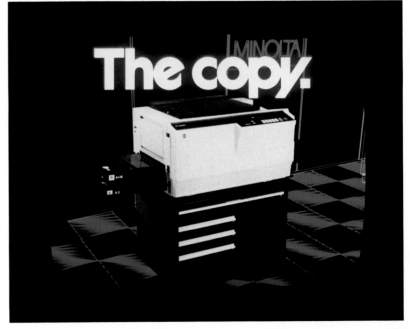

Facility identification and a neon sign in Ginza, Tokyo

Identifizierung von Herstellungsstätten und Neonbeleuchtung bei Ginza, Tokyo

Identification des lieux et enseigne au néon à Ginza, Tokyo

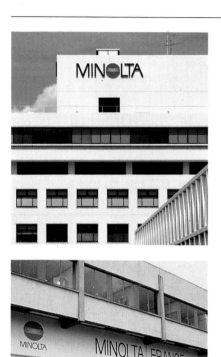

■ ⟨⊹⟩ SBB CFF FFS

Design: Müller-Brockmann + Co.
in cooperation with Peter Spalinger

Design: Müller-Brockmann + Co.
Mitarbeit Peter Spalinger

Design: Müller-Brockmann + Cie
Collaboration Peter Spalinger

The New Visual Information System for Railway Stations and Stops of the Swiss Federal Railways

Buildings of public traffic, which are much frequented, do cause the user manifold problems of orientation. Today's complicated situation in railway stations, the capacity of which is utilized to the extreme, and within which various traffic systems are combined, require clearly designed, visual means of communication. SBB ordered the advertising and design agency Müller-Brockmann + Co., Zürich, to work out directives for a uniform orientation system for all railway stations and stops in Switzerland, which as a partial concept should later on be integrated into an overall visual appearance of SBB.
In close cooperation with the building construction branch of SBB General Management, Müller-Brockmann + Co. developed a design handbook to serve as final directive for all new direction signs in railway stations. This comprehensive concept — an assembly kit — was tested in practice at the Olten railway station, which was to get new signs — and they were judged as being good. For the time being, it contains the following elements:
– typeface and symbol concept
– shape and color of the information signs
– application and combination method of the individual information elements

Das neue visuelle Informationssystem für Bahnhöfe und Stationen der Schweizerischen Bundesbahnen

Bauten des öffentlichen Verkehrs mit hohen Besucherfrequenzen bringen für den Benützer vielfältige Orientierungsprobleme. Die heutigen komplizierten Situationen in den bis aufs letzte ausgenützten Bahnhöfen und das Zusammenkommen verschiedener Verkehrssysteme erfordern klar gestaltete visuelle Kommunikationsmittel. Die Werbe- und Designagentur Müller-Brockmann + Co., Zürich, erhielt von den SBB den Auftrag, Richtlinien zu erarbeiten für ein einheitliches Orientierungssystem für alle Bahnhöfe und Stationen der Schweiz, welche sich später als Teilkonzept in ein gesamtes visuelles Erscheinungsbild der SBB integrieren lassen.
In enger Zusammenarbeit mit dem Hochbaudienst der Generaldirektion SBB erarbeitete Müller-Brockmann + Co. ein Gestaltungshandbuch als verbindliche Richtlinie für alle neu zu schaffenden Wegweisungen in den Bahnhöfen.
Dieses umfassende Konzept – ein Baukastensystem – wurde in der Praxis – im neu zu beschriftenden Bahnhof Olten – getestet und für gut befunden. Es enthält vorläufig folgende Elemente:
– Schrift und Bildzeichenkonzept
– Form und Farbe der Informationsträger
– Anwendungs- und Kombinationsmethode der einzelnen Informationselemente

Le nouveau système d'information visuelle pour gares et stations des Chemins de fer fédéraux

Les bâtiments des transports publics, avec leur fréquence élevée de voyageurs, engendrent de multiples problèmes d'orientation pour l'usager. Face aux situations souvent complexes qui surgissent dans les gares exploitées au maximum de leurs capacités et situées au point de convergence de divers systèmes de transport, une conception claire des moyens de communication visuelle s'avère indispensable. L'agence de publicité et de design Müller-Brockmann + Cie, Zurich, a été chargée par les CFF de développer un système d'orientation cohérent pour toutes les gares et stations CFF, qui pourraient être intégrées plus tard, sous forme de concepts partiels, dans une image d'identification visuelle globale.
En étroite collaboration avec la Division des bâtiments de la Direction générale des CFF, un manuel de conception formelle a été réalisé: il contient les lignes directrices régissant la création de tout nouveau système d'orientation dans les gares. Cette conception globale, fondée sur le principe du système modulaire, a été testée dans la pratique pour le nouveau système d'orientation de la gare d'Olten. L'essai a été concluant. La conception globale se compose actuellement des éléments suivants:
– caractères typographiques et symbole
– forme et couleur des supports d'information
– méthode d'application et de combinaison des différents éléments d'information

Orientation of today's railway customers is now guaranteed in that
- information elements, their combination method, shape and color always appear alike
- the means of information at the points of decision are arranged in a way that they take into consideration the flow of traffic and the structural environment

Today's guidelines again contain some old, proven elements in a slightly modified manner. Moreover, the guidelines of the International Railway Association, UIC, were taken into consideration.

The graphic element, like the signet and the new pictograms, the arrow, the typeface and the colors also apply to the rolled-on time schedules and to the poster time tables in the entire SBB building.

Die Orientierung der heutigen Bahnkunden ist nun dadurch gewährleistet, dass
- die Informationselemente, deren Kombinationsmethode, die Form und Farbe stets gleichartig erscheinen
- die Informationsmittel an den Entscheidungspunkten so angeordnet sind, dass sie auf den Verkehrsfluss und die bauliche Umgebung Rücksicht nehmen.

In den heutigen Richtlinien sind einige alte, bewährte Elemente etwas modifiziert wieder enthalten. Zudem wurden die Richtlinien des Internationalen Eisenbahnverbandes UIC berücksichtigt.

Die grafischen Elemente wie Signet und die neuen Piktogramme, der Pfeil, die Schrift und die Farben gelten sinngemäss auch für das Rollmaterial sowie die Anschriften im gesamten Baubereich der SBB.

L'information des voyageurs est aujourd'hui assurée grâce à
- une présentation toujours identique des éléments d'information, de la combinaison de ces éléments, de la forme et des couleurs,
- une disposition des moyens d'information en des points névralgiques, compte tenu du flux des voyageurs et des constructions voisines.

Les nouvelles lignes directrices reprennent divers éléments anciens, dûment éprouvés, en les modifiant quelque peu. Par ailleurs, les directives de l'Union internationale des chemins de fer (UIC) ont été prises en considération.

Les éléments graphiques, tels que l'emblème et les nouveaux pictogrammes, la flèche, les caractères et les couleurs, trouvent application au même titre, tant pour le matériel roulant que pour les inscriptions dans tout le secteur des bâtiments CFF.

The New Handbook "Visual Information System in Railway Stations and Stops" of SBB

Das neue Handbuch «Visuelles Informationssystem in Bahnhöfen und Stationen» der SBB

Le nouveau manuel «Système d'information visuelle dans les gares et stations de chemins de fer» des CFF

Because of this problematic arrow shape, the SBB signet has a very limited function in the overall orientation system. The signet may only be used as a building label together with the city name of the railway station, and/or in relation with the SBB building. In the future the signet will always appear negatively behind a red or black background.

Within a screen, pictograms and direction arrows are designed as a uniform visual concept. The picture itself was taken from the UIC standards.

The direction arrow always appears as a superimposed "symbol" and therefore without a small frame as against all other symbols (pictograms).

The pictograms serve as elements of direction to mark businesses or places and are always shown within a small frame. Signals which indicate movement, were used pointing to the left and to the right. They must always be arranged to follow the arrow.

The texts in the signs are always written in Helvetica sanserif bold type.

Das SBB-Signet hat in dem gesamten Orientierungssystem aufgrund seiner problematischen Pfeilform nur eine ganz beschränkte Funktion. Das Zeichen darf nur als Gebäudeanschrift, zusammen mit dem Ortsnamen des Bahnhofes bzw. der Funktion des SBB-Gebäudes, Verwendung finden. Das Signet erscheint in Zukunft immer negativ im roten bzw. im schwarzen Feld.

Piktogramme und Richtungspfeile werden innerhalb eines Rasters als einheitliche visuelle Konzeption gestaltet. Der Bildinhalt wurde aus den UIC-Normen übernommen.

Der Richtungspfeil erscheint immer als übergeordnetes «Zeichen» und deshalb gegenüber allen andern Bildzeichen (Piktogrammen) ohne Rähmchen. Die Piktogramme dienen als Elemente der Wegweisung zur Kennzeichnung von Lokalen oder Anlagen und erscheinen immer in einem Rähmchen. Nicht richtungsneutrale Bildsymbole, das heisst solche, die eine Bewegung darstellen, wurden in einer Links- (nach links) und einer Rechtsrichtung (nach rechts) verwendet. Sie sind immer in Pfeilrichtung anzuordnen.

Für die Texte in den Schildern wird ausschliesslich die Helvetica Grotesk halbfett verwendet.

Le sigle CFF n'a qu'une fonction très restreinte dans l'ensemble du système d'orientation, à cause de sa configuration fort problématique en forme de flèche. Le symbole ne peut être utilisé que pour les inscriptions sur les bâtiments, conjointement avec le nom de la gare, resp. la fonction du bâtiment des CFF. A l'avenir, le sigle apparaîtra toujours en négatif sur fond rouge, resp. noir.

Les pictogrammes et les flèches de direction sont réalisés en tant que conception visuelle uniforme dans le cadre d'une trame donnée. Le contenu de l'image est repris des normes UIC.

La flèche de direction apparaît toujours comme «symbole générique» et n'est de ce fait pas encadrée comme tous les autres pictogrammes.

Les pictogrammes servent d'éléments informatifs pour désigner un local ou une installation: ils sont toujours présentés dans un petit cadre. Les symboles qui ne sont pas «neutres» du point de vue de l'orientation ont été utilisés dans un sens bien déterminé: ils sont orientés soit vers la gauche, soit vers la droite. Ils doivent toujours être disposés dans le sens de la flèche.

Pour les textes sur les écriteaux, l'on a utilisé exclusivement les caractères antiques Helvetica mi-gras.

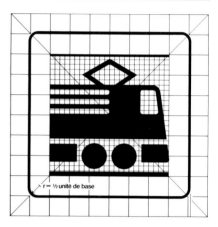

r = ½ unité de base

Gleis
1

r = ½ Grundeinheit

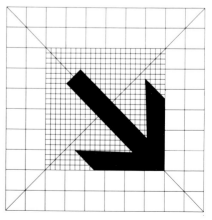

The typeface sizes for all signs were reduced to 3, whereby within one display of signs only one size may be used. In order to secure legibility even from far away, the distance between letters was stipulated. Mixed lettering is used consistently, i.e. capitals and small letters in each case.
All signs of the orientation system are

Die zu verwendenden Schriftgrössen für alle Schilder wurden auf 3 reduziert, wobei innerhalb einer Schilderanlage nur eine Grösse verwendet werden darf. Der Buchstabenabstand wurde genau festgelegt, um die Lesbarkeit auch auf weite Distanzen zu gewährleisten. Es wird konsequent die gemischte Schreibweise angewendet,

La gradation des corps des caractères destinés aux écriteaux a été réduite à 3 catégories. Une seule et même force de corps peut être utilisée pour une même série d'écriteaux. L'espacement des caractères a été déterminé avec précision afin d'assurer une bonne lisibilité, même sur de grandes distances. Des majuscules et des minus-

made of the traditional color blue. In order to secure the largest possible contrast to the white typeface the dark blue used previously was selected (ultra marine blue RAS 5002). The signet always appears on the red field (traffic red RAL 3020).
Off-limit labels and all buildings and facilities not meant to be entered by railway customers are made of white letters on a black background.
The signs are made of enamel.

also in jedem Fall Gross- und Kleinbuchstaben.
Sämtliche Schilder des Orientierungssystems werden in der traditionellen blauen Farbe ausgeführt. Um den Kontrast zur weissen Schrift möglichst gross zu halten, wurde das bisher verwendete dunkle Blau gewählt (Ultramarinblau RAL 5002).
Das Signet erscheint immer auf dem roten Feld (Verkehrsrot RAL 3020). Dienstanschriften und alle Gebäude und Lokale, die nicht für den Bahnkunden bestimmt sind, werden in Schwarz mit weisser Schrift ausgeführt.
Die Schilder werden in Email ausgeführt.

cules ont été utilisées conjointement et de manière systématique.
Tous les écriteaux du système d'orientation sont tenus dans la couleur bleue traditionnelle. Pour obtenir un contraste aussi prononcé que possible par rapport aux caractères blancs, l'on a choisi le bleu foncé utilisé jusqu'à ce jour (outremer RAS 5002).
Le sigle apparaît toujours sur fond rouge (rouge signal RAL 3020).
Les inscriptions de service, ainsi que les inscriptions sur tous les bâtiments et locaux non destinés aux voyageurs, sont exécutées en caractères blancs sur fond noir.
Les écriteaux sont en émail.

The Basel Railway Station

So far, a portion of the signs at the Basel Railway Station was made following the new labelling concept. In the newly constructed subways illuminated signs are also used.

Bahnhof Basel

Für den Bahnhof Basel wurde bis jetzt ein Teil der Schilder aufgrund des neuen Beschriftungskonzeptes ausgeführt. In den neu ausgebauten Unterführungen werden auch hinterleuchtete Schilder verwendet.

La gare de Bâle

Pour la gare de Bâle, une partie des écriteaux a été réalisée jusqu'ici sur la base de la nouvelle conception de communication visuelle. Dans les passages souterrains nouvellement aménagés, des écriteaux éclairés depuis l'arrière sont également utilisés.

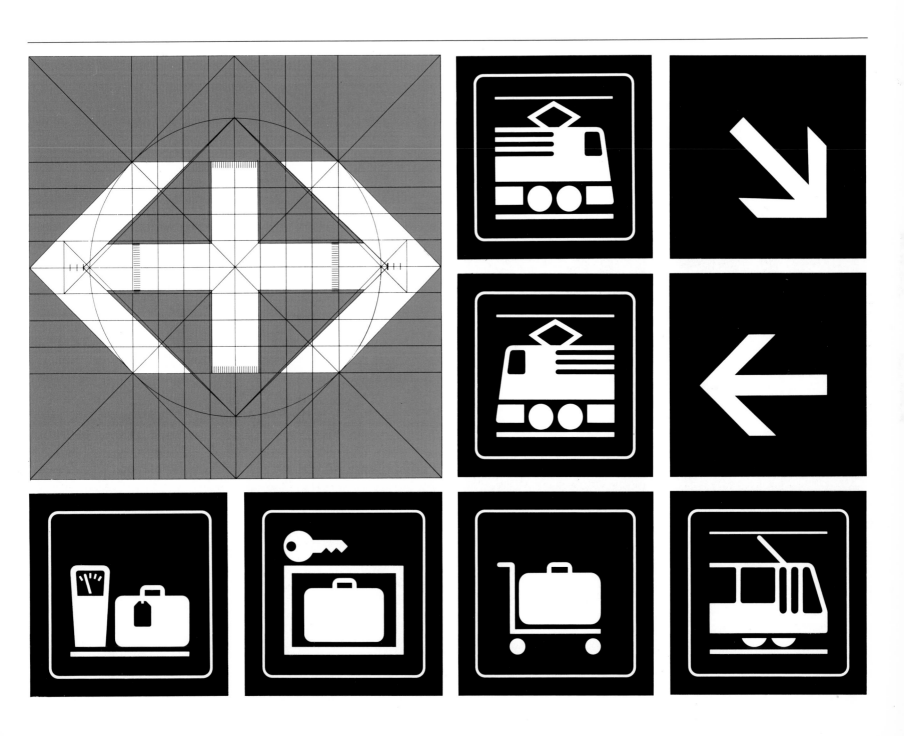

Gr=G|r □= fünf Einheiten / cinq unités   re = r|e □= eine Einheit / une unité

A B C D E F G H I J K L M
N O P Q R S T U V W X Y Z
a b c d e f g h i j k l m
n o p q r s t u v w x y z
1 2 3 4 5 6 7 8 9 0

Grenchen Süd

5 1 4 4 4 4 4 ½ Versalhöhe 4 4

The Olten Railway Station
The New Orientation System in the Olten Railway Station

- As a "novelty", repeated city signs on the platforms
- Numbering of platforms
- Directions in subways
- Newly designed departure and direction signs above the stairs leading to the subways
- Application of signet and logo on the new rolling indicators
- Labelling of an SBB building

Bahnhof Olten
Das neue Wegweisungssystem im Bahnhof Olten

- Als «Neuheit» sich wiederholende Ortsschilder auf den Perrons
- Gleisnumerierung
- Wegweisung in den Unterführungen
- Neu gestaltete Abfahrtsanzeiger und Richtungsanzeiger über den Treppenabgängen zu den Unterführungen
- Anwendung des Signets mit dem Logo auf dem neuen Rollmaterial
- Beschriftung einer SBB-Einrichtung

La gare d'Olten
Le nouveau système d'orientation de la gare d'Olten

- En tant qu'«innovation», répétition sur chaque quai des écriteaux indiquant le nom de la localité
- Numérotation des voies ferroviaires
- Panneaux d'orientation dans les passages souterrains
- Indicateurs de départ et de direction, de conception nouvelle, au-dessus des descentes d'escalier menant aux passages souterrains
- Application du sigle avec le logo sur le nouveau matériel roulant
- Inscription sur une installation CFF

Identification on corporate items

Identifizierung, unternehmensbezogen

Identification spécifique de l'entreprise

A New Time-Table and a New Face for the Swiss Federal Railways

By Markus Seger, Manager of Advertising Services of the Swiss Federal Railways

Ein neuer Fahrplan und ein neues Gesicht für die Schweizerischen Bundesbahnen

Markus Seger, Chef des Werbedienstes der Schweizerischen Bundesbahnen

Un nouvel horaire et un nouveau visage pour les Chemins de fer fédéraux

De Markus Seger, chef du Service de publicité des Chemins de fer fédéraux

---

A public transportation system must primarily perform public service in a customer-friendly manner.

No wonder, therefore, that a railway system primarily seeks its optical identity in the area of everyday confrontation with the customer.

The previous chapter showed, how the Swiss Federal Railways tackled this problem. Beyond this, does a railway still need an optical profile as an enterprise? Or is this endeavour merely narcissism?

It needs it. — In particular, in a country like Switzerland where the "Swiss Federal Railways" share the national railway system with more than 100 private railways about half and half.

The SBB CFF FFS — as the Federal Railways are abbreviated in the languages of the country — in 1982 had to especially rely on appearing as a dynamic modern enterprise characterized by a clear handwriting and signature.

This year in its entire network they have introduced the rhythmic timetable at one hour intervals and a 10–30% increase of train riding incentives.

Instituting a modern marketing system, a new company policy and the slogan "new orientation of the company" are further examples of the company's self-identification.

This way, 1982 — the year of the introduction of the rhythmic time-table — became the first year of a new Corporate Identity of the Swiss Federal Railways.

Ein öffentliches Verkehrsmittel hat in erster Linie den öffentlichen Dienst in kundenfreundlicher Form zu leisten.

Kein Wunder also, wenn eine Eisenbahn ihre visuelle Identität zuallererst im Bereich der täglichen Begegnung mit dem Kunden sucht.

Wie die Schweizerischen Bundesbahnen diese Aufgabe angegangen sind, ist im vorangehenden Kapitel beschrieben.

Braucht eine Bahn darüber hinaus noch ein optisches Profil als Unternehmung? Oder ist dieses Bestreben blosser Narzissmus?

Sie braucht. – Besonders in einem Land wie die Schweiz, wo sich die «Schweizerischen Bundesbahnen» mit über 100 Privatbahnen etwa hälftig ins nationale Bahnnetz teilen.

Die SBB CFF FFS – wie die Bundesbahnen in den drei Landessprachen abgekürzt und sprachüblich bezeichnet werden – waren 1982 in besonders starkem Masse auf eine Profilierung als dynamische moderne Unternehmung mit klarer Handschrift und Unterschrift angewiesen.

In diesem Jahr haben sie auf ihrem gesamten Netz den Taktfahrplan mit Stundentakt und eine 10- bis 30prozentige Steigerung des Zugsangebotes eingeführt.

Die Institutionalisierung eines modernen Marketing, eine neue Unternehmungspolitik und das Schlagwort «Neuorientierung der Unternehmung» setzten weitere Zeichen der unternehmerischen Selbstfindung.

So wurde 1982 – das Jahr der Einführung des Taktfahrplans – zum ersten Jahr einer neuen Corporate Identity der Schweizerischen Bundesbahnen.

Un moyen de transport public doit tout d'abord assurer le service public aux clients avec tact et prévenance.

Faut-il s'étonner, dès lors, que les chemins de fer cherchent tout d'abord à exprimer leur identité visuelle dans les rencontres quotidiennes avec les clients?

La manière dont les Chemins de fer fédéraux se sont attaqué à cette tâche a fait l'objet d'une description dans le précédent chapitre.

Faut-il, en plus, qu'une compagnie des chemins de fer ait un profil visuel en tant qu'entreprise? Ou bien une telle tentative est-elle uniquement l'expression d'une attitude narcissiste?

Le profil est indispensable – surtout dans un pays comme la Suisse où les «Chemins de fer fédéraux» se partagent le réseau national de moitié avec quelque 100 chemins de fer privés.

Les CFF SBB FFS (telle est la désignation et l'abréviation habituelle des Chemins de fer fédéraux dans les trois langues nationales) devaient en 1982 se profiler tout particulièrement comme entreprise dynamique moderne, avec une écriture et une signature traduisant clairement leur personnalité.

C'est en effet en 1982 que les CFF ont introduit l'horaire cadencé prévoyant des intervalles d'une heure, ainsi qu'une augmentation de 10–30% de l'offre en trains sur leur réseau.

L'institutionnalisation d'un marketing moderne, la nouvelle politique d'entreprise et le slogan de la «réorientation de l'entreprise» ont constitué d'autres jalons dans la recherche de la personnalité de l'entreprise.

L'année 1982 – année d'introduction de l'horaire cadencé – est ainsi devenue la première année d'une nouvelle Corporate Identity des Chemins de fer fédéraux.

Opening of the change in rhythm. A give-away catalogue with recollection label on the front page. The new locomotive bears the introduction date as a number.

Auftakt zum Taktwechsel. Ein Streuprospekt mit Erinnerungskleber auf der Vorderseite. Die neue Lokomotive trägt das Einführungsdatum als Nummer.

Introduction de l'horaire cadencé. Prospectus de grande diffusion avec collant-souvenir appliqué au recto. La nouvelle locomotive porte la date d'introduction en guise de numéro.

**1982:
Wir fahren mit Takt.**

So heisst unser Motto 1982.

Ab 23. Mai 1982 fahren wir auch im Takt. Denn ab 23. Mai 1982 bieten wir Ihnen 30% mehr Intercity- und Schnellzugsverbindungen.

Und ab 23. Mai 1982 haben Sie mindestens jede Stunde eine gute Verbindung in jede Richtung.

1982 werden Sie mit Ihrer SBB auch sonst viel Neues erleben.

1982 sollten Sie sich darum vor jeder Reise fragen, reise ich im Zug oder fahre ich selber?

Aus Vernunft werden Sie sich diese Frage stellen. Und wir hoffen gerne, dass sie Ihnen 1982 keine Ruhe lässt.

Gute Reise.

Wir fahren mit Takt.

 Ihre SBB

From the campaign started by the advertising agency Young & Rubican, Bern, to introduce the new rhythmic time-table: two-page magazine advertisement playing with words: *"with* rhythm / *in* rhythm".

Aus der von der Werbeagentur Young & Rubicam, Bern, gestalteten Kampagne zur Einführung des Taktfahrplans: Doppelseitige Zeitschriftenanzeige mit dem deutschen Wortspiel «*mit* Takt / *im* Takt».

Extrait de la campagne conçue par l'agence de publicité Young & Rubican, Berne, pour l'introduction de l'horaire cadencé: double-page avec le jeu de mots allemand: «*mit* Takt / *im* Takt» (avec tact / en cadence).

Further examples from the introductory campaign for the rhythmic timetable of the Swiss Federal Railways. Consistent application of uniform typefaces and of uniform sender designation at sufficient design freedom.

Weitere Beispiele aus der Einführungskampagne für den Taktfahrplan der Schweizerischen Bundesbahnen. Konsequente Anwendung einheitlicher Schriften und der einheitlichen Absenderbezeichnung bei genügend gestalterischem Freiraum.

Autres exemples de la campagne d'introduction pour l'horaire cadencé des Chemins de fer fédéraux. Utilisation systématique de types de caractères uniformes et d'une désignation uniforme de l'entreprise, avec une large liberté d'action accordée au créateur graphique.

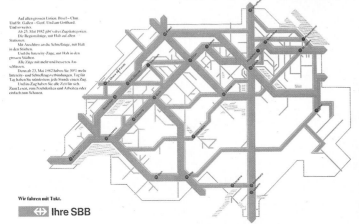

Wir fahren mit Takt.

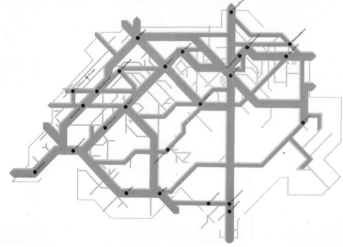

Jetzt täglich ab Solothurn:

17 x **Basel**
56 x **Bern**
34 x **Biel**
24 x **Burgdorf**
16 x **Genf**
17 x **Zürich**

Wir fahren mit Takt.

⬦ Ihre SBB

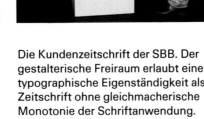

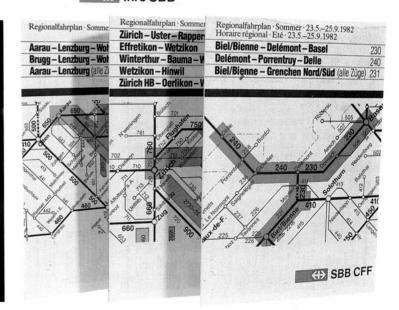

The customer magazine of SBB. The design freedom allows for typographic individuality as a magazine without equalizing monotony of typeface application.

Die Kundenzeitschrift der SBB. Der gestalterische Freiraum erlaubt eine typographische Eigenständigkeit als Zeitschrift ohne gleichmacherische Monotonie der Schriftanwendung.

Le bulletin d'information du CFF. La liberté d'action du graphiste permet une conception typographique autonome du bulletin, sans tomber dans la monotonie et l'uniformisation.

133

Advertising at the point of sale: consistently used graphic elements at simultaneous adjustment to the character of the medium and of environment.

Werbung am Verkaufspunkt: konsequent durchgezogene grafische Elemente bei gleichzeitiger Anpassung an den Charakter des Mediums und der Umgebung.

Publicité au point de vente: éléments graphiques appliqués systématiquement, avec adaptation judicieuse au caractère du média et à l'environnement.

Planning Director: Motoo Nakanishi
Design Director: Yutaka Sano
Coordinator: Isao Kageyama
Design: PAOS Inc.

Direktor der Planung: Motoo Nakanishi
Direktor der Gestaltung: Yutaka Sano
Koordinator: Isao Kageyama
Gestaltung: PAOS Inc.

Directeur de planification: Motoo Nakanishi
Directeur de design: Yutaka Sano
Coordinateur: Isao Kageyama
Conception: PAOS Inc.

Development of a Corporate Identity (CI) System and Brand Strategy for the Trio-Kenwood Corporation

Entwicklung einer Firmenidentität und Markenstrategie für die Trio-Kenwood Corporation

Développement d'une identité d'entreprise et d'une stratégie de marque pour la Trio-Kenwood Corporation

The Trio-Kenwood Corporation was established in 1946 and is today well known throughout the world as an audio specialist manufacturer. The name Trio was adapted as both a corporate and product name in recognition of the company's three original founders.

However, as of 1964, when the company first moved into the American market, distributors in that market proposed that Kenwood be introduced as an international brand name. However, the Trio brand name remains in use in Japan and England.

In 1980 PAOS, the corporate identity consulting firm, was called upon to develop a new corporate identity system.

PAOS began tackling the problem by conducting surveys and analyses of management in general. Problem areas were then detected and new management plans proposed in the eight areas of corporate ideals, corporate systems and organization, the market, products, sales, services and the problems of dealing with communication.

These factors were wholeheartedly accepted by management. Work on the project then proceeded to the stage of developing a new design system and design element as the focal point of the new image strategy. The first line of action for this image strategy was to switch from using the two corporate brands, Trio and Kenwood, to just Kenwood in the international market. The second was to develop design elements and a system that would always create a sense of high quality, progressiveness and smartness — these are the three key image words.

Die Trio-Kenwood Corporation wurde 1946 gegründet und ist heute weltweit als Spezialfirma für Tongeräte bekannt.

Der Name Trio wurde in Anerkennung der drei Gründer sowohl als Firmen- als auch als Produktbezeichnung angenommen.

Als die Firma jedoch 1964 erstmals in den amerikanischen Markt eindrang, schlugen die Importeure auf diesem Markt vor, Kenwood als internationale Markenbezeichnung zu benützen. Die Bezeichnung Trio wird jedoch in Japan und England weiterverwendet.

1980 wurde PAOS, eine Beratungsfirma in Fragen Unternehmensidentität, aufgefordert, eine neue Identität für Trio-Kenwood zu schaffen.

PAOS startete das Projekt mit Untersuchungen und Analysen vom Management im allgemeinen. Es wurden Problemfelder herauskristallisiert und in den acht Bereichen von Unternehmensidealen, Firmensystemen und Organisation, Markt, Produkte, Verkäufe, Kundendienst und dem Problem der Behandlung der Kommunikation Managementpläne vorgeschlagen. Diese Faktoren wurden vom Management voll akzeptiert. Die Arbeit an dem Projekt ging dann in das Stadium der Entwicklung eines neuen Gestaltungssystems und Gestaltungselements als Kernpunkt der Strategie für ein neues Erscheinungsbild. Der erste Zug in dieser Strategie war die Abwendung von den beiden Markenbezeichnungen Trio und Kenwood und die blosse Verwendung von Kenwood auf dem internationalen Markt. Der zweite Schritt war die Entwicklung eines Gestaltungselementes und eines Systems, das immer ein Gefühl von hoher Qualität, Fortschrittlichkeit und Klugheit vermitteln würde – dies sind die drei Schlüsselbegriffe für das Erscheinungsbild.

La Trio-Kenwood Corporation, fondée en 1946, jouit aujourd'hui d'une notoriété mondiale en tant que spécialiste du «son». L'appellation Trio, à la fois raison sociale et désignation des produits, a été adoptée en l'honneur des trois fondateurs de la société. Toutefois, lorsqu'en 1964 l'entreprise pénétra pour la première fois sur le marché américain, les distributeurs proposèrent l'introduction de Kenwood en tant que marque de produits internationale. La marque Trio continue toutefois d'être utilisée au Japon et en Grande-Bretagne. En 1980, l'entreprise conseil PAOS a reçu mandat de développer une nouvelle image d'identification de l'entreprise. PAOS s'est attaqué au problème en effectuant tout d'abord des enquêtes et des analyses de la gestion en général. Puis, les secteurs problématiques ont été détectés et de nouveaux plans de direction proposés dans huit secteurs spécifiques: les idéaux de l'entreprise, les systèmes et l'organisation, le marché, les produits, les ventes, les services, les communications. Ces propositions ont été pleinement acceptées par la direction de l'entreprise. L'élaboration détaillée des projets a finalement abouti au développement d'un nouveau système et d'un nouvel élément de conception formelle en tant que point focal de la nouvelle stratégie d'identification. La première série de mesures dans le cadre de cette nouvelle stratégie visait à réduire les deux marques d'entreprise, Trio et Kenwood, à une seule marque internationale: Kenwood. Le second pas consistait à développer un système d'esthétique industrielle susceptible d'exprimer l'idée de haute qualité, de progrès et de bonne facture, c'est-à-dire les trois éléments-clés de l'image d'identification.

トリオ株式会社

TRIO-KENWOOD CORPORATION

The most important aspect of this new corporate identity system was to coordinate on a visual image level the improvements and progress achieved by such electronic techniques as miniaturization, enhanced effectiveness and performance of products and the emergence of digital audio technology.

With these fundamental plans accepted, PAOS then proposed four final design candidates from which the present design was chosen. The new corporate identity was announced at a press meeting in Japan in September 1982. Since then, details of the basic design system along with the development and introduction of various application design systems have been gradually added. In Japan, England and some other commonwealth countries, the introduction of this new corporate identity will take some time due to the brand change from Trio to Kenwood required of existing products. To complement the new design, a new Trio logotype was created. However this is strictly a supplementary element for use until the changeover is completed. The Trio-Kenwood Corporation has three other operational divisions apart from that concerned with audio products. These are communications equipment (ham radios, etc.), testing instruments (oscilloscopes, etc.), and records. The various brands of these divisions will also be unified under the brand name of Kenwood.

Der wichtigste Aspekt dieses neuen Systems einer Firmenidentität war, die Verbesserungen und den Fortschritt durch elektronische Techniken, wie Kleingeräteherstellung, höhere Produktwirkung und -leistung und die Entwicklung der Audiodigitaltechnologie, auf visuelle Weise darzustellen. Nachdem diese Grundlagenpläne akzeptiert waren, schlug PAOS vier endgültige Gestaltungsvarianten vor, von denen die gegenwärtige Form ausgesucht wurde. Die neue Unternehmensidentität wurde anlässlich einer Pressekonferenz in Japan im September 1982 vorgestellt. Seither wurden dann bestimmte Einzelheiten der Grundgestaltung parallel zur Entwicklung und Einführung von verschiedenen Anwendungsgestaltungssystemen nach und nach hinzugefügt. In Japan, England und einigen anderen Commonwealth-Ländern dauerte die Einführung dieser neuen Unternehmensidentität aufgrund der Namensänderung von Trio zu Kenwood bei den bestehenden Produkten eine geraume Zeit. Um die neue Gestaltung zu ergänzen, wurde ein neues Trio-Logo geschaffen. Jedoch ist dies, genaugenommen, nur ein Austauschelement, das nur so lange verwendet wird, bis der Wandel vollzogen ist. Die Trio-Kenwood Corporation hat ausser dem Tongerätebereich drei weitere Betriebszweige. Es handelt sich dabei um Übertragungsgeräte (Amateurradios usw.), Versuchsgeräte (Oszillographen usw.) und Schallplatten. Die verschiedenen Marken dieser Bereiche werden ebenfalls in die Markenbezeichnung Kenwood integriert werden.

Le plus important aspect de ce nouveau système d'identité de l'entreprise était de coordonner, au niveau de l'image visuelle, les améliorations et progrès accomplis dans les technologies électroniques telles que la miniaturisation, l'amélioration de l'efficacité et des performances des produits, ainsi que le développement de la technologie audio-digitale.

Une fois ces plans de base acceptés, PAOS proposa quatre variantes de conception définitives, parmi lesquelles fut choisie la forme actuellement appliquée. La nouvelle identité d'entreprise fut annoncée à une conférence de presse en 1982 au Japon. Depuis, divers éléments de conception formelle ont été ajoutés au système, parallèlement avec le développement et l'introduction de diverses variantes d'application.

Au Japon, en Grande-Bretagne et dans quelques autres pays du Commonwealth, l'introduction de la nouvelle image d'identification prendra quelque temps en raison de la nécessité de passer de la marque Trio, actuellement utilisée, à celle de Kenwood. Pour compléter la nouvelle conception formelle, un nouveau logotype Trio a été créé. Celui-ci n'est en fait qu'un élément de transition, jusqu'à ce que le changement de marque soit complètement achevé. La Trio-Kenwood Corporation a trois autres secteurs d'activité, à savoir: équipement de communication (radio pour amateurs T.S.F., etc.), instruments d'essai (oscilloscopes, etc.) et disques. Les marques divergentes de ces trois secteurs seront également unifiées en une seule: Kenwood.

TRIO

Characteristics of New Design Elements and their System

Kennzeichen der neuen Gestaltungselemente und deren System

Caractéristiques des nouveaux éléments de conception visuelle et de leur système

To heighten the attractiveness and recognition factors of the logotype while at the same time maintaining its legibility, a triangle was placed above the ''W'' creating a focal point in the centre of the long brand name, Kenwood. To make the most of this design characteristic, a systematic and flexible approach to form was taken to suit each product and item. This was achieved by applying a colour change to the triangular part of the basic logotype.

Um die Anmutung und Wiedererkennung des Logos zu erhöhen und gleichzeitig die Leserlichkeit zu erhalten, stellte man über das «W» ein Dreieck und schuf somit einen Kernpunkt in der Mitte der langen Markenbezeichnung. Um aus diesem Gestaltungsmerkmal das meiste zu machen, ging man an die Form systematisch und flexibel heran, damit sie jedem Produkt und Artikel gerecht wurde. Dies gelang durch farbliche Veränderung an dem Dreieck des eigentlichen Logos.

Pour renforcer l'attractivité et la valeur de réminiscence du logotype, tout en maintenant sa parfaite lisibilité, un triangle a été placé au-dessus du «W», structurant ainsi la longueur de la marque Kenwood en lui conférant un point focal en son centre. Pour rehausser encore l'aspect caractéristique de cette conception, une approche systématique et flexible a été choisie, en adoptant une forme typique pour chaque produit ou article. Ce résultat a été atteint en changeant la couleur de l'élément triangulaire du logotype de base.

KENWOOD

The triangle is extended at its upper edge, and as a sub-element represents a condensed image of the spreading of sound. Modified stripes have also been designed as an additional element. This sub-element in particular is used when a visual form of promotion is required, which is quite easy to see from the design of the application items.

Das Dreieck ist nach oben verlängert und stellt als Unterelement ein zusammenfassendes Bild vom Ausbreiten des Klanges dar. Als weiteres Element kamen veränderte Streifen hinzu. Dieses Subelement wird besonders dann verwendet, wenn Werbung in visueller Form erforderlich wird, die von der Gestaltung der Anwendungsbeispiele leicht erkennbar ist.

Ce triangle se prolonge dans la partie supérieure et représente, en tant que sous-élément, une image condensée de la propagation du son. Des rayures modifiées ont également été conçues comme élément additionnel. Ce sous-élément est plus spécialement utilisé lorsqu'on recherche une forme de promotion visuelle facile à identifier, comme le montrent les différentes variantes des exemples d'application.

KENWOOD
KENWOOD

トリオ株式会社
TRIO-KENWOOD CORPORATION

The characteristic of the colour system is to show as clearly as possible the relationship between the figure and the background and to give the image of precision that is required of the products. If possible, yellow should be used for the sub-element triangle and the logotype triangle, while it is specified that the letters of the logotype and background should be a monochrome gradation from white to black or a colourless silver, etc.

Das Farbsystem soll die Beziehung zwischen dem Gestalteten und dem Hintergrund so deutlich wie möglich darstellen und ein Bild der Genauigkeit vermitteln, die die Geräte besitzen müssen. Wenn möglich, sollte Gelb für das Subelement Dreieck und das Logodreieck verwendet werden, während festgesetzt wurde, dass die Buchstaben des Logos und Hintergrundes monochrom von Weiss zu Schwarz abfallen oder in einem farblosen Silberton usw. gehalten werden.

Le système de couleurs exprime clairement la relation entre la figure et le fond de l'image, et donne une idée du haut degré de précision des appareils. Si possible, le jaune doit être utilisé pour le sous-élément triangulaire et le triangle du logotype, alors que, selon les spécifications, les lettres du logotype et le fond doivent être tenus en des coloris monochromes allant graduellement du blanc au noir ou au ton argent incolore, etc.

1 Audio lab range	1 Audiolaborserie	1 Série d'appareils audios
2 Digital audio record player	2 Digitalaudioplattenspieler	2 Tourne-disque audio-digital
3 Receiver	3 Empfänger	3 Récepteur
4 Car radio	4 Autoradio	4 Autoradio
5 Video cassette tapes	5 Videokassettenbänder	5 Bandes vidéo-cassettes
6 Packaging	6 Verpackungskarton	6 Carton d'emballage

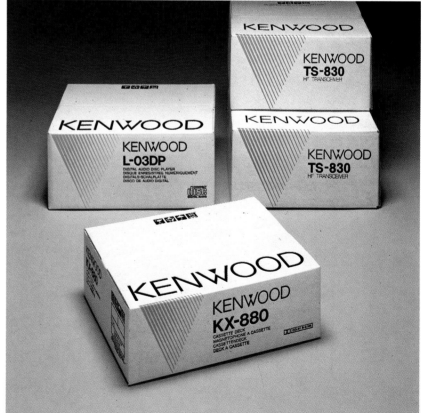

1 Record
2 Record cover
3 Carrying bag

1 Schallplatte
2 Schallplattenumschlag
3 Tragtasche

1 Disque
2 Enveloppe de disque
3 Cabas

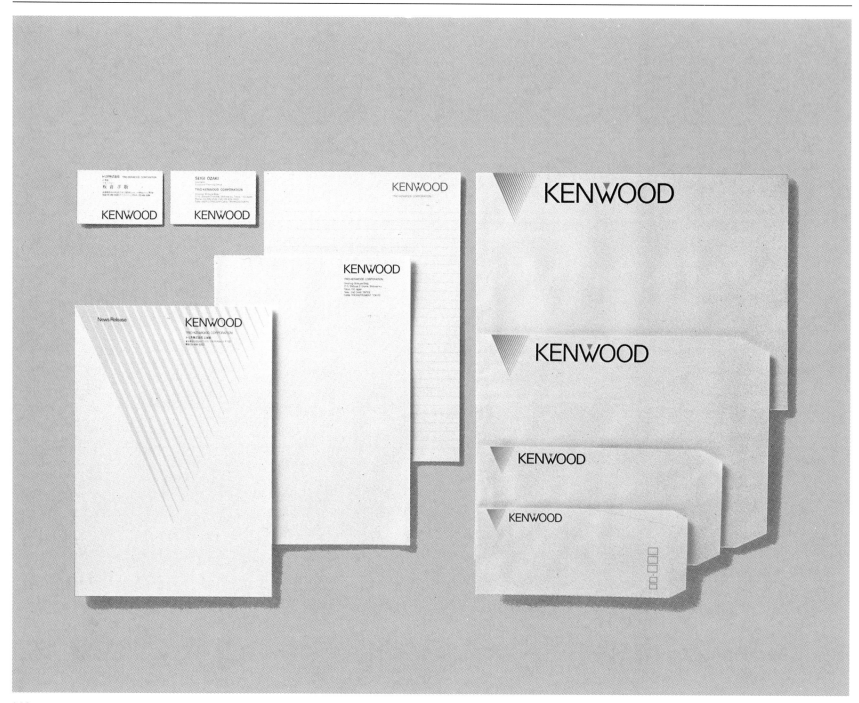

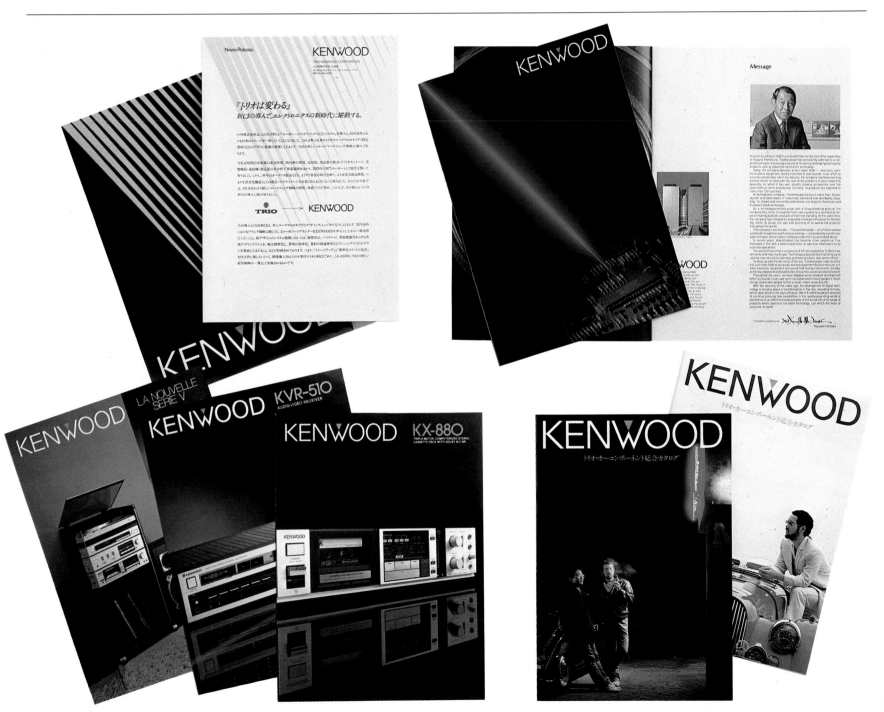

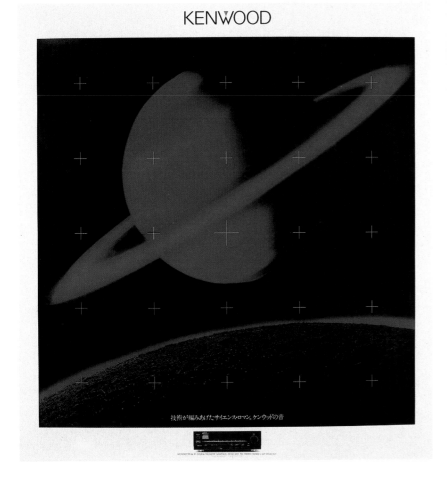

New Factory:

1 The exterior
2 The conveyor assembly

Neue Fabrik:

1 Das Äussere
2 Förderband

Nouvelle fabrique:

1 Aspect extérieur
2 Bande de transport

1 Sound studio
2 Maintenance cars

1 Vorführungsstudio
2 Wartungsautomobile

1 Studio de démonstration
2 Voitures d'entretien

BodaNova.

Design: Signe Persson-Melin
         Mikael Björnstjerna
Product Development Manager:
Anders Färdig
Marketing Manager: Ralph Theander

Boda Nova
The Idea that Turned into a Company

Boda Nova
Die Idee, die zum Unternehmen wurde

Boda Nova
Une idée devenue entreprise

It started in the closing years of the sixties. Sweden's most historic glass manufacturer — Kosta Boda — started, together with the designers Signe Persson-Melin and Mikael Björnstjerna and the art director John Melin, to draw up the first plans for a new project which had the working name of "Good Things".
The need was felt to turn the thoughts about functional products for the table into a more concrete, advanced and timeless design of high quality. Parallel with the production of glass the desire had long been felt for a channel for ideas that were not directly applicable to the material of glass. At their disposal there were a number of excellent resources: ideas, gifted designers, marketing competence and last (not least) the good reputation of Boda glass.
So after intensive years of preparation the first Boda Nova collection was introduced to the market in the spring of 1971 with a range including products of stoneware, heat-resistant glass, cork and wood — materials that had in many cases not previously been used for tableware. The materials were thus revolutionary, but above all it was the design that was to prove itself representative of a new way of thinking. The simple; the strict; the functional; the timeless.

Es begann in den letzten Jahren der Sechziger. Schwedens ältester Glashersteller – Kosta Boda –, gemeinsam mit den Gestaltern Signe Persson-Melin und Mikael Björnstjerna sowie dem Grafiker John Melin, machte die ersten Pläne für ein neues Projekt, das den Namen «Good Things» erhielt.
Sie fühlten das Bedürfnis, die Überlegungen über funktionelle Produkte für den Tisch in einen konkreteren, fortschrittlicheren und zeitlosen Entwurf hoher Qualität zu verwandeln. Parallel zur Glasherstellung hat man lange den Wunsch gehegt, Kanäle für Gedanken zu finden, die auf das Material Glas nicht direkt anwendbar waren. Ihnen stand eine ganze Anzahl ausgezeichneter Quellen zur Verfügung: Ideen, talentierte Gestalter, ein fähiges Marketing und nicht zuletzt der gute Name von Boda-Glas.
So wurde im Frühjahr 1971 nach Jahren intensiver Vorbereitung die erste Boda-Nova-Kollektion auf den Markt gebracht. Die Serie schloss Artikel aus Steingut, hitzebeständigem Glas, Kork und Holz ein – Materialien also, die in vielen Fällen zuvor nicht für Tischgeschirr verwendet worden waren. Die Materialien waren somit bahnbrechend, aber in erster Linie war es die Gestaltung, die eine neue Denkungsart vertrat. Das Einfache, das Genaue, das Funktionelle, das Zeitlose.

L'histoire commença vers la fin des années soixante. La plus ancienne verrerie suédoise – Kosta Boda – entreprit, avec le concours des designers Signe Persson-Melin et Mikael Björnstjerna, ainsi que de John Melin, directeur artistique, d'élaborer ses premiers plans pour un nouveau projet appelé «Good Things».
Le besoin s'était fait sentir de traduire les considérations générales sur des articles de table fonctionnels en une conception de haute qualité, plus concrète, plus progressiste et échappant aux contingences d'un engouement momentané. Parallèlement à la production d'articles en verre avait surgi le désir de pouvoir réaliser des idées créatrices en d'autres matériaux, chaque fois que le verre ne convenait pas. D'excellentes possibilités et ressources s'offraient à nous: idées, créateurs doués, compétence de marketing et, enfin, la bonne réputation dont jouit la verrerie Boda.
Après des années de préparation intense, la première collection Boda Nova a été lancée sur le marché au printemps 1971, ensemble avec toute une gamme de produits en grès, verre résistant aux hautes températures, liège et bois. L'usage de ces matériaux était révolutionnaire. Mais c'était avant tout le design qui était l'expression d'une nouvelle esthétique industrielle, où l'accent était mis sur une conception simple, stricte, fonctionnelle, classique.

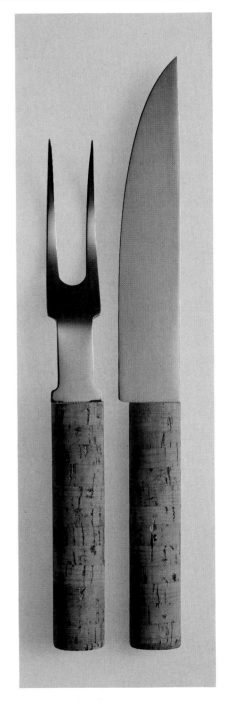

Simplicity— a Philosophy

Einfachheit – eine Philosophie

La simplicité – une philosophie

The consistent idea, the idea that bears up the whole of the Boda Nova project is a classic simplicity of colour and lines. A concept with an origin that can be traced back to the flow of ideas behind functionalism, and which may be seen as an extension of the now classic Bauhaus design, which decreed purity in a design that is a product of its time. A first glance at a Boda Nova product can give an impression almost of anonymity. It never flatters the eye with unnecessary details and patterns. The Boda Nova range is also notable, with its strict simplicity, as never being launched specifically either for everyday use or for special occasions.
A delight for the eye—a pleasure for the hand … this product philosophy provides much of the feeling that is meant to be conveyed with the whole of the idea "Boda Nova". The choice of material for the various products is therefore a subject of particular interest. The designer chooses his materials for a specific reason and for the purpose to which they are best suited. Boda Nova was an early pioneer in the field of innovative design for the table-top market. Cork and heat-resistant glass were therefore materials that they were the first to introduce to the market. Cork had previously been nothing but insulating material.

Die konsequente Idee, die Idee, die das ganze Boda-Nova-Projekt trägt, ist eine klassische Einfachheit von Farbe und Linie. Ein Konzept mit einem Ursprung, der auf die Gedankenströme zum Funktionalismus zurückgeführt werden kann und das als Erweiterung der heute klassischen Bauhausgestaltung, die einem Produkt ihrer Zeit in der Gestaltung Reinheit gab, gesehen werden darf. Ein erster Blick auf ein Boda-Nova-Produkt hinterlässt fast den Eindruck von Anonymität. Es schmeichelt dem Auge nie durch unnötige Einzelheiten und Muster. Es ist darüber hinaus bemerkenswert, dass die Boda-Nova-Produkte in ihrer unbedingten Einfachheit nie speziell zum Alltagsgebrauch oder für besondere Gelegenheiten auf den Markt gebracht werden.
Eine Freude für das Auge – ein Genuss für die Hand… Diese Produktphilosophie überträgt viel von dem Gefühl, das mit der ganzen Idee Boda Nova übertragen werden soll. Die Auswahl des Materials für die verschiedenen Produkte ist deshalb ein Thema von besonderem Interesse. Der Gestalter wählt sein Material aus einem bestimmten Grund und nach dem Zweck, für das es sich am besten eignet. Boda Nova war einer der ersten Pioniere auf dem Gebiet erfinderischer Gestaltung von Tafelgeschirr. Kork und wärmebeständiges Glas waren deshalb Materialien, die erstmals von dieser Firma auf dem Markt eingeführt wurden. Kork war vorher nichts als Isoliermaterial.

L'idée fondamentale qui est à la base de l'ensemble du projet Boda Nova est celle de la simplicité classique des couleurs et des lignes. Ce concept, dont les origines remontent jusqu'aux courants d'idées caractéristiques du fonctionnalisme, peut être considéré comme une extension des principes désormais classiques du Bauhaus, selon lesquels un produit conforme au goût de son temps pèche par manque de pureté. Au premier abord, les produits Boda Nova donnent quasiment une impression d'anonymité. Aucun détail, aucun effet ornemental ne vient flatter le regard. Il convient aussi de relever que les produits Boda Nova, avec la simplicité rigoureuse de leurs lignes, n'ont jamais été spécifiquement propagés ni comme articles d'usage courant, ni comme réservés aux grandes occasions.
Un enchantement au regard – un plaisir au toucher…, cette philosophie des produits exprime bien les sentiments que la conception globale «Boda Nova» entend communiquer. Le choix des matériaux pour les différents produits acquiert de ce fait une importance toute particulière. L'artiste choisit chaque matériau pour une raison bien déterminée et en fonction de ses propriétés spécifiques. L'entreprise Boda Nova a fait œuvre de pionnier dans la création de concepts innovateurs pour les articles de table. Elle a été la première à lancer sur le marché des produits en liège et en verre réfractaire aux hautes températures. Jusque-là, le liège était uniquement connu comme matière isolante.

A Range with an Exclusive Selection

Eine Produktpalette mit exklusiver Auswahl

Une gamme de produits raffinés

Boda Nova's product range is unique, in that it notes extremely few changes from year to year and takes in a remarkably small number of new items in the annual presentation of its collection, compared with the rest of its competitors.

For the most part the basic range remains unchanged since the beginning of the seventies—as good a proof as any that good design has a value that cannot be eroded by time. An example of the sort of product that the company produces to meet a particular need is the Gourmet spoon (see picture). New French cooking, "La Nouvelle Cuisine", produces food for which normal conventional cutlery sometimes proves lacking: sauces and purées, for example, require suitable implements in order to be relished to the full.

Consideration for and interest in food of every shape is consistently part of the Boda Nova concept. Food must express itself—not its forcefully attractive surroundings. So many of the names behind the products have themselves been food experts.

The designer Signe Persson-Melin is, apart from her design work, also a formidable cook and the woman behind many of the popular recipe booklets provided by Boda Nova.

Boda Novas Produktpalette ist einmalig, indem sie von Jahr zu Jahr extrem wenige Veränderungen bringt und im Vergleich mit der Konkurrenz eine beachtenswert kleine Anzahl neuer Artikel in der alljährlich neuen Kollektion präsentiert.

Im wesentlichen ist die Grundpalette seit Anfang der siebziger Jahre unverändert geblieben – vielleicht der beste Beweis, dass gute Gestaltung einen Wert hat, der sich über die Zeit nicht abträgt. Ein Beispiel für die von dem Unternehmen hergestellten Produkte ist der Feinschmeckerlöffel (siehe Abbildung). In der neuen französischen Küche, «La Nouvelle Cuisine», werden Gerichte zubereitet, für die das normale herkömmliche Besteck zu wünschen übriglässt: Sossen und Purées zum Beispiel erfordern geeignetes Handwerkzeug, um voll genossen werden zu können.

Achtung für und Interesse an Essen in jeder Form ist ein konsequentes Element des Boda-Nova-Konzeptes. Ein Gericht muss für sich selbst sprechen – nicht das erzwungen attraktive Drumherum. So viele der Persönlichkeiten, die hinter dem Produkt stehen, sind selbst Feinschmecker.

Die Gestalterin Signe Persson-Melin ist neben ihrer gestalterischen Tätigkeit eine erstklassige Köchin, und sie ist die Dame, die hinter vielen der beliebten kleinen Rezeptbücher steht, die von Boda Nova zur Verfügung gestellt werden.

La gamme des produits Boda Nova est unique en ce sens qu'elle ne connaît que de très rares changements d'une année à l'autre et que, comparée à la concurrence, elle n'ajoute qu'un très petit nombre de nouveaux articles à la collection qu'elle présente chaque année. Dans l'ensemble, la gamme de base est pratiquement restée inchangée depuis le début des années soixante-dix. C'est peut-être là la meilleure preuve que la valeur inhérente à une bonne création visuelle ne peut pas se dégrader avec le temps. Un exemple du genre de produits conçus par l'entreprise pour répondre à un besoin spécifique est la cuillère Gourmet (voir reproduction). «La Nouvelle Cuisine» produit des mets pour lesquels les couverts traditionnels ne conviennent pas: les sauces et purées, par exemple, exigent des instruments appropriés pour celui qui veut en déguster toute la saveur.

«L'art de bien manger» sous toutes ses formes constitue une partie importante de la nouvelle conception Boda Nova. Un met doit plaire par lui-même, et non pas par les aspects nécessairement plaisants qui l'entourent.

Signe Persson-Melin est non seulement une excellente graphiste et un remarquable cordon-bleu, mais encore l'auteur qui – avec une sensibilité typiquement féminine – a rédigé bon nombre des petits volumes de recettes diffusés par Boda Nova.

An Eye Outwards and to the Future

Ein Blick nach aussen und in die Zukunft

Le regard tourné vers le marché international et l'avenir

Boda Nova's platform has slowly but surely, sensibly and expertly been built firm in its domestic market. It has already total market coverage where this is sought.

With solid experience of the products and understanding of its customers' needs and wishes, eyes are turned cautiously to the future. Not least the international market suggests exciting possibilities for further development of the ascetic Boda Nova profile.

Boda Novas Plattform wurde auf dem Inlandsmarkt langsam, aber sicher vernünftig und fachgemäss fest aufgebaut. Boda Nova beherrscht, wo die Produkte gebraucht werden, den Markt in vollem Masse.

Mit solider Produkterfahrung und Verständnis für die Bedürfnisse und Wünsche des Kunden wirft man jetzt einen vorsichtigen Blick auf die Zukunft. Nicht zuletzt sieht es so aus, als böte der internationale Markt stimulierende Möglichkeiten für eine Weiterentwicklung des asketischen Boda-Nova-Profils.

Boda Nova ne s'est établi que lentement sur le marché national, mais avec assurance, sensibilité et «en connaisseur». L'entreprise atteint aujourd'hui une couverture totale du marché partout là où elle recherche cet objectif.

Grâce à ses profondes connaissances des produits et à sa compréhension pour les besoins et désirs des clients, Boda Nova se tourne désormais vers l'avenir, avec toute la prudence requise. Le marché international semble, en effet, offrir des perspectives fascinantes pour le futur développement du profil ascétique de Boda Nova.

Marketing via Selected Customers in Sweden and for Export

Marketing über erlesene Kunden in Schweden und für den Export

Un marketing fondé sur des clients soigneusement sélectionnés

Soufflé. Lätt. Gott. Roligt.

Signe Persson-Melin ger recept.

Simple, deliciously fresh food.

Salad recipes from Boda Nova.

One of the ideas behind Boda Nova's basic philosophy is that the range be marketed at home in Sweden and for export via a limited selection of customers who must sell the complete programme. In this way the product idea is preserved and communicated in the best manner. Since all the different items belong to one another and have a mutual relationship the total concept should also be marketed in its entirety.

Einer der Gedanken hinter Boda Novas grundlegender Philosophie ist, dass die Produktpalette zu Hause in Schweden verkauft wird und zusätzliche Exportgeschäfte über eine begrenzte Auswahl von Kunden getätigt werden, die das komplette Produktprogramm verkaufen müssen. Auf diese Weise bleibt die Produktidee erhalten und wird am besten weitervermittelt. Da all die verschiedenen Produkte zueinander gehören und eine gegenseitige Beziehung zueinander haben, sollte auch das Gesamtkonzept als eine Einheit weitergegeben werden.

Une des idées fondamentales de la philosophie de Boda Nova est de commercialiser toute la gamme des produits destinés au marché suédois et à l'exportation, grâce à des clients chargés de vendre le programme complet. Etant donné que les différents produits forment un tout et qu'il existe des relations mutuelles entre eux, il convient de les commercialiser sous forme de concept global.

Eldfast glas.

Heat-resistant glass. BodaNova Sweden

Trä.

Wood. BodaNova Sweden

Kork.

Cork. BodaNova Sweden

Stengods.

Stoneware. BodaNova Sweden

Metall.

Metal. BodaNova Sweden

Porslin.

Porcelain. BodaNova Sweden

Unique
Agency Collaboration

Konsequente
Agenturarbeit

Collaboration unique
avec l'agence
de publicité

One of the most important marketing strengths is a uniform and consistent line in display material, packaging, advertising, posters and so on. The graphic design of all Boda Nova material is strict and clear — the type face is always the same and completely in line with the Boda idea in Futura Upright.
Posters and shop display material are based to a large extent on highly qualified illustrations. Display material is produced on high-class material and can be used later on further occasions — it is timeless and independent of current trends.

Eine der wichtigsten Stärken des Marketings ist ein einheitliches und konsequentes Auftreten durch Ausstellungsmaterial, Verpackung, Werbung, Plakate usw. Die grafische Gestaltung aller Boda-Nova-Elemente ist scharf umrissen und klar – das Schriftbild ist immer das gleiche und entspricht voll der Boda-Idee des «Futura upright». Plakate und Schaufenstermaterial basieren weitgehend auf qualitativ hochwertigen Illustrationen. Ausstellungsmaterial wird auf erstklassigen Werkstoffen erstellt und kann bei späteren Gelegenheiten weiterverwendet werden – es ist zeitlos und unabhängig von Zeitströmen.

Une des exigences essentielles du marketing est la présentation conséquente et cohérente de l'entreprise à travers le matériel d'exposition, le conditionnement, la publicité, les affiches, etc. La conception graphique de tous les éléments Boda Nova est strictement définie; les caractères typographiques concordent avec l'idée de Boda Nova sur la Futura Upright. Les affiches et le matériel d'exposition se fondent largement sur des illustrations de haute qualité. Ils sont réalisés en matériaux de premier choix et sont de conception classique.

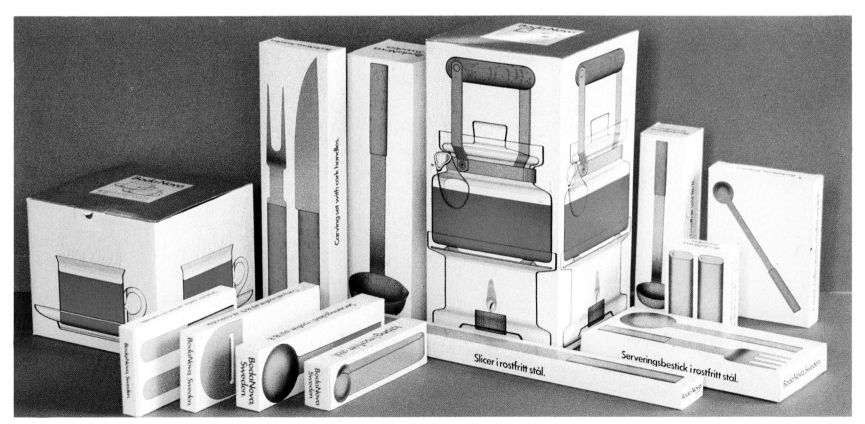

As an integrated and extremely important partner in marketing and product development one of Sweden's largest and generally acknowledged leading advertising agencies, Arbmans in Malmö, have been involved from the start. This almost unique collaboration gives scope for new ideas and the necessary development while keeping its eye constantly to the original philosophy.

Eine der in Schweden grössten und allgemein als führend anerkannten Werbeagenturen, Arbmans in Malmö, war von Anfang an als wesentlicher und äusserst wichtiger Partner für Marketing und Produktentwicklung dabei. Diese fast einmalige Zusammenarbeit lässt Raum für neue Ideen und für die notwendige Weiterentwicklung, wobei die ursprüngliche Philosophie nie aus den Augen gelassen wird.

L'agence de publicité Arbmans à Malmö, une des plus grandes agences suédoises qui joue un rôle prépondérant sur le marché national, a été associée à Boda Nova dès le départ en tant que partenaire responsable du marketing et du développement des produits. Cette collaboration quasi unique laisse place aux idées nouvelles et aux perfectionnements indispensables, sans jamais perdre de vue la philosophie originale.

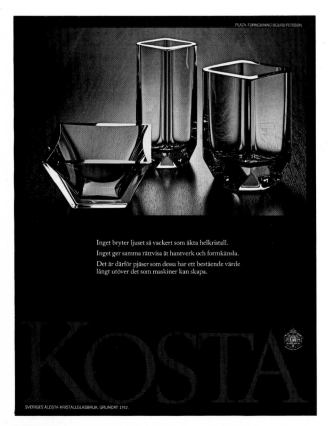

Inget bryter ljuset så vackert som äkta helkristall.
Inget ger samma rättvisa åt hantverk och formkänsla.
Det är därför pjäser som dessa har ett bestående värde långt utöver det som maskiner kan skapa.

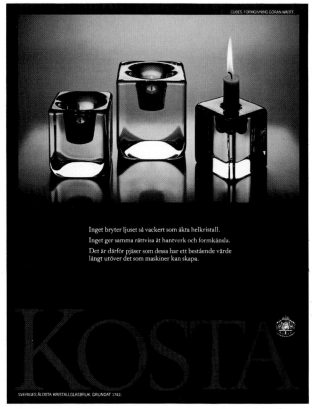

Inget bryter ljuset så vackert som äkta helkristall.
Inget ger samma rättvisa åt hantverk och formkänsla.
Det är därför pjäser som dessa har ett bestående värde långt utöver det som maskiner kan skapa.

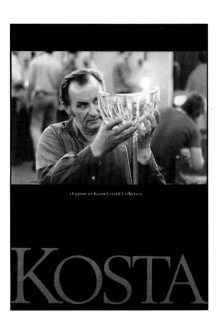

EL AL ישראל

Design: Dan Reisiger

EL AL—Israel's Bridge to the World

EL AL – Israels Brücke zur Welt

EL AL – un pont entre Israël et le monde

The creation of a corporate identity in response to a series of corporate needs arising within the various departments of a company over a period of years is a challenge which requires steadfastness of purpose and some optimism on the part of the designer. The new corporate identity developed for El Al, Israel's national airline, was achieved in just such a manner — as a slowly evolving process in which each stage was viewed individually by each department head, rather than as part of a unified design intention. It was the responsibility of the designer to develop and maintain his design concept from project to project.

Die Schaffung einer Unternehmensidentität als Antwort auf eine Reihe von Unternehmensbedürfnissen, die innerhalb der verschiedenen Abteilungen eines Unternehmens über die Jahre hinweg entstehen, ist eine Herausforderung, die von seiten des Gestalters Zielstrebigkeit und einigen Optimismus erfordert. Auf genau solche Weise wurde die neue Identität für El Al, Israels nationale Fluglinie, entwickelt – als ein sich langsam entwickelnder Prozess, in dem jedes Stadium individuell von jedem Abteilungsleiter betrachtet wurde und nicht als Teil einer einheitlichen Gestaltungsabsicht. Es war die Verantwortung des Gestalters, sein gestalterisches Konzept von Projekt zu Projekt zu entwickeln und einzuhalten.

La création d'une identité d'entreprise en réponse à toute une série de besoins spécifiques qui se sont manifesté au sein des différents départements tout au long des années, constitue non seulement un défi lancé au créateur graphique, mais exige de l'artiste qu'il se porte vers l'objectif visé avec ardeur et une bonne dose d'optimisme. La nouvelle CI développée pour El Al, la compagnie aérienne nationale d'Israël, a été créée dans cet esprit, en tant que processus d'évolution dans lequel chaque étape constituait non seulement un élément partiel d'une conception formelle globale, mais était l'objet d'une considération individuelle par le préposé de chaque département. Le «concepteur» était responsable de l'élaboration et de l'application de la conception graphique globale d'un projet à l'autre.

Design Philosophy

Gestaltungsphilosophie

La philosophie de la création graphique

The concept we developed for El Al was based on the consideration that a corporate identity has to serve the company's goals and reflect its potential and capability. Design can influence the development of a company, but the design is ultimately a mirror of the company's excellence.

The major design projects for El Al were carried out during its most vital and dynamic years.

From the first we had a new totality in mind and were convinced of the need to create a new corporate identity based on the new logo — even if the company itself was not yet aware.

The design projects that eventually evolved into a ten-year long design process were:

1 Creation of a unified Hebrew/Latin logo as part of the 747 livery design and environmental graphics for its interior
2 Design of passenger service items, catering items, brochures, etc.
3 Design of ground equipment markings and accompanying manual
4 Design of final version of unified logo and flag — company signature
5 Design of the company's stationery with its manual
6 Design of 737 and 767 aircraft livery and interior

Das Konzept, das wir für El Al entwikkelten, basierte auf der Überlegung, dass eine Unternehmensidentität den Zielen der Firma dienen und deren Möglichkeiten und Fähigkeiten reflektieren muss. Durch Gestaltung kann die Entwicklung einer Firma beeinflusst werden, aber die Gestaltung ist letztendlich ein Spiegel der Exzellenz eines Unternehmens.

Die hauptsächlichen Gestaltungsprojekte von El Al wurden während der lebhaftesten und dynamischsten Jahre des Unternehmens durchgeführt.

Von Anfang an dachten wir an eine neue Gesamtheit und waren von der Notwendigkeit überzeugt, es müsse eine neue Identität auf der Basis des Logos geschaffen werden – selbst wenn dem eigentlichen Unternehmen dies noch nicht bewusst war.

Die Gestaltungsprojekte, die sich schliesslich zu einem zehnjährigen Gestaltungsprozess entwickelten, waren im einzelnen:

1 Schaffung eines einheitlichen hebräisch/lateinischen Logos in Übereinklang mit der Gestaltung der Dienstkleidung für die 747 und deren grafische Innenausstattung
2 Gestaltung von Passagierserviceartikeln, Artikeln der Lebensmittelversorgung, Broschüren usw.
3 Gestaltung von Markierungen für die Bodenausrüstung und eine begleitende Handschrift
4 Gestaltung der endgültigen Version des Logos und der Fahne – Firmenunterschrift
5 Gestaltung der Firmenbriefbögen mit dem entsprechenden Handbuch
6 Gestaltung von Dienstkleidung und Innenausstattung für die 737- und 767-Flugzeuge

La conception que nous avons développée pour El Al se fonde sur l'idée qu'une identité d'entreprise doit se placer au service des objectifs visés et refléter les possibilités et les capacités de l'entreprise. Le travail de création graphique peut influencer le développement d'une société, mais il est en dernier ressort le miroir qui réfléchit les valeurs réelles de l'entreprise.

Les principaux projets de conception formelle d'El Al ont été réalisés pendant les années les plus animées et les plus dynamiques de l'entreprise.

Dès le départ, nous avions à l'esprit une nouvelle conception globale et étions convaincus de la nécessité de créer une nouvelle identité sur la base du logotype, même si l'entreprise en tant que telle n'avait pas encore pris conscience de cette exigence.

Les projets de conception formelle, qui ont finalement été développés dans le cadre d'un processus étalé sur dix ans, sont les suivants:

1 Création d'un logo intégré hébreu/latin, en conformité avec la conception de l'uniforme de l'équipage et de l'aménagement intérieur du Boeing 747
2 Conception des articles de service à l'usage des passagers, denrées alimentaires, brochures, etc.
3 Conception du marquage de l'équipement au sol, ainsi que d'un manuel explicatif
4 Elaboration de la version définitive du logotype de la compagnie et de l'emblème «amiral»
5 Conception du papier à lettres, ainsi que du manuel correspondant
6 Conception des uniformes de l'équipage et de l'aménagement intérieur des avions 737 et 767.

Intuitive Corporate Expression

Intuitiver Unternehmensausdruck

Expression intuitive de la personnalité de l'entreprise

When El Al was founded shortly after the establishment of the State of Israel in 1948, very little was thought about the logotype or corporate identity. There was, however, an intuitive statement of pride about the very existence of a Jewish national airline, which immediately found expression in the decoration of the tails of all the aircraft with the Israeli flag, which consists of blue and white stripes and the six-point Star of David.
This was — and is — a strong visual statement of "keep the flag flying", which will remain with El Al, while design policies may come and go.

The Hebrew Alphabet
Despite the fact that the Hebrew alphabet is not a universal medium of communication, it would have been unthinkable to omit it from the national airline's signature. A solution had to be found to maintain the Hebrew logo at the same level of visual expression as the Latin character logo, and at the same time create in internationally recognizable communication.

Als die El Al kurz nach Gründung des Staates Israel im Jahre 1948 ins Leben gerufen wurde, dachte man sehr wenig an das Logo oder an Unternehmensidentität. Es gab jedoch den gefühlsmässigen Ausdruck von Stolz auf das blosse Vorhandensein einer jüdischen nationalen Luftlinie, der sofort in der Dekoration des Hecks aller Flugzeuge mit der israelischen Flagge Ausdruck fand, die aus blauen und weissen Streifen und dem sechszackigen Stern von David besteht.
Dies war – und ist – ein starker visueller Ausdruck von «lasst die Flagge fliegen», der bei El Al bleibt, während Gestaltungsstrategien vielleicht kommen und gehen.

Das hebräische Alphabet
Obwohl das hebräische Alphabet kein universelles Kommunikationsmedium ist, so wäre es doch undenkbar, es aus der Unterschrift der nationalen Fluglinie herauszulassen. Es musste eine Lösung gefunden werden, das hebräische Logo auf derselben Ebene visuellen Ausdrucks wie das Logo in lateinischen Buchstaben zu halten, wobei es galt, gleichzeitig eine international erkennbare Kommunikation zu schaffen.

Lorsque El Al a été fondée en 1948, peu après la création de l'Etat d'Israël, l'on ne pensait guère au logotype ou à l'identité de l'entreprise. C'est le sentiment de fierté d'avoir sa propre compagnie aérienne nationale juive qui s'est intuitivement et spontanément exprimé par l'application, sur l'aileron de tous les avions, du pavillon national israélien composé de rayures bleues et blanches et de l'étoile de David à six pointes.
C'était là, et c'est aujourd'hui encore, l'expression visuelle percutante de la volonté de «hisser les pavillons en bannière» qui reste immuablement attachée à El Al, alors que les stratégies de design changent et évoluent.

L'alphabet hébreu
Bien que l'alphabet hébreu ne soit pas un moyen de communication universel, il aurait été impensable de ne pas l'intégrer à l'emblème de la compagnie aérienne nationale. Il fallait trouver un moyen pour maintenir le logo hébreu au même niveau d'expression visuelle que le logo avec les caractères latins, tout en créant une forme de communication universellement reconnaissable.

Evolving Concept of Identity

Entstehendes Konzept einer Identität

Le concept d'identité en évolution

A Bridge

Israel's geo-political situation has placed the national airline in the position of being the symbol of a bridge between the country and the rest of the world. The integrated Hebrew/Latin character logo, with its two way readability — Hebrew from right to left, and the Latin characters from left to right — served to create an image of a bridge between the two cultures and transformed the national to an international visual communication.

The difficulty we experienced in adapting the two square logos to an elongated area induced us to create a new logo integrating the two alphabets into a single statement. The new integrated logo was immediately accepted by the management for the 747 livery though no thought was given to its further application. We were convinced of the necessity to introduce it as the logo for the entire company and realized its potential as a cornerstone for a new corporate identity program.

When the head of the catering division invited us to design the items for passenger food service, we exploited the opportunity to repeat the new logo and the orangepink-red color scheme that we had already introduced to the 747 interior.

This was followed by the ground equipment division.

Eine Brücke

Israels geopolitische Situation hat die nationale Fluglinie in die Lage versetzt, das Symbol einer Brücke zwischen dem Land und der übrigen Welt zu sein. Das integrierte hebräisch/lateinische Logo mit seiner zweifachen Lesbarkeit – hebräisch von rechts nach links und lateinisch von links nach rechts – schuf die Vorstellung einer Brücke zwischen den beiden Kulturen und verwandelte die nationale in eine internationale visuelle Kommunikation.

Die Schwierigkeiten, auf die wir bei dem Versuch, die zwei quadratischen Logos an eine verlängerte Oberfläche anzupassen, stiessen, veranlassten uns, ein neues Logo zu schaffen, in dem die beiden Alphabete in eine einzige Aussage integriert wurden.
Das neue integrierte Logo wurde von der Geschäftsleitung sofort für die Dienstkleidung der 747 akzeptiert, obwohl man in keiner Weise an weitere Anwendungen dachte. Wir waren von der Notwendigkeit überzeugt, es als Logo für das gesamte Unternehmen einzuführen, und waren uns seiner Möglichkeiten als Eckpfeiler für ein neues Programm für die Unternehmensidentität bewusst.
Als der Leiter der Verpflegungsstation uns aufforderte, die Artikel für die Verpflegung der Passagiere zu gestalten, nutzten wir die Gelegenheit, das neue Logo und das orange-rote Farbschema, das wir bereits bei der Ausstattung der 747 eingeführt hatten, zu wiederholen.
Dieses Beispiel wurde von der Abteilung für Bodengeräteausstattung weiterverfolgt.

Un pont

La situation géopolitique d'Israël a amené la compagnie aérienne nationale à prendre valeur de symbole, d'un pont jeté entre le pays et le reste du monde. Le logo intégré hébreu/latin, avec ses deux sens de lecture (l'hébreu est lu de droite à gauche, les caractères latins de gauche à droite) a permis de créer l'image du pont qui relie deux formes de culture, transformant ainsi le symbole national en un signe international de communication visuelle.

Les difficultés rencontrées lors de notre tentative d'adapter les deux logos carrés à la surface allongée du gouvernail nous ont incité à créer un nouveau logotype intégrant les deux alphabets en une seule et même forme d'expression.
Le nouveau logo intégré a été immédiatement accepté par la direction générale pour les uniformes de l'équipage du Boeing 747, bien qu'on ne songeait alors guère à d'autres formes d'application. Or, nous étions convaincu de la nécessité d'introduire le logo comme symbole pour l'ensemble de l'entreprise et d'en faire la pierre angulaire du programme fondé sur la nouvelle identité d'entreprise.
Lorsque le préposé du service d'approvisionnement nous a chargé de la conception des articles destinés à l'approvisionnement des passagers, nous avons profité de cette opportunité pour reprendre le nouveau logo, ainsi que la gamme des coloris orange-rose-rouge, déjà utilisés pour l'aménagement du 747.
L'exemple fut suivi par le service responsable de l'équipement au sol.

When creating the manual for this division, we again took the opportunity to incorporate the new logo and to redesign the colors of the ground equipment from olive green and cobalt blue to fresh green, sky blue and white, in keeping with the new livery. A small manual containing minimum instructions and maximum examples was published. This resulted in quick and easy implementation.
The El Al ground equipment livery subsequently won an international award in Chicago in 1974.

Als das Handbuch für diese Abteilung erstellt wurde, nahmen wir nochmals die Gelegenheit wahr, das neue Logo einzubauen, und gestalteten die Farben der Bodenausstattung von Olivegrün und Kobaltblau in ein frisches Grün, Himmelblau und Weiss um und blieben auch bei der neuen Dienstkleidung dabei. Ein kleines Handbuch mit minimalen Richtlinien und maximalen Beispielen wurde veröffentlicht. Dies führt zu einer schnellen und problemlosen Durchführung.
Die Dienstkleidung von El Al für das Bodenpersonal gewann später 1974 einen internationalen Preis in Chicago.

Lorsque nous avons créé le manuel destiné à ce service, nous avons à nouveau profité de l'occasion pour introduire le nouveau logotype et pour remplacer les couleurs vert olive et bleu cobalt de l'équipement au sol par des tons vert clair, bleu ciel et blanc qui harmonisent mieux avec les nouveaux uniformes de l'équipage. Un petit manuel a été publié, contenant un minimum d'instructions et un maximum d'exemples pratiques. Il a grandement facilité l'application de la nouvelle conception graphique.
Un prix international a été décerné à El Al en 1974 à Chicago pour l'uniforme de son personnel au sol.

It was at this point that the company management realized that it had a new corporate identity that had evolved over a period of time, and that there was no turning back. In 1979 we were commissioned to create a logo-type and stationery manual, thus finally establishing the new integrated logo and new color schemes as mandatory for all company divisions as of 1 January 1980.

A corporate identity expressing Israel's national pride and history, the region's sun and colors and the company's global operations had been established.

With the introduction of the Boeing 747 to the El Al fleet, we were commissioned to design the aircraft livery and environmental graphics for the interior.

The Sun
El Al also identified itself with the country's famous Mediterranean sun. When designing the environmental graphics for the Boeing 747 jumbo aircraft, we based the color scheme on the image of the sun — orange, pink, red, silver and white — in keeping with the company's wish to welcome passengers to the warm colors of Israel.

An diesem Punkt angelangt, bemerkte die Geschäftsleitung des Unternehmens, dass es eine neue Unternehmensidentität besass und dass es davon kein Zurück mehr gab. Im Jahre 1979 wurden wir beauftragt, eine Handschrift über die Schriftart des Logos und der Briefbögen herauszugeben, wodurch schliesslich mit Wirkung vom 1. Januar 1980 ein neues integriertes Logo und neue Farbschemen als zwingend für alle Unternehmensabteilungen erstellt wurden. Eine Unternehmensidentität war geboren, die Israels Nationalstolz und seine Geschichte, die Sonne und Farben der Landschaft und die weltweite Tätigkeit des Unternehmens widerspiegelt.

Bei Einführung der Boeing 747 bei El Al erhielten wir den Auftrag für die Gestaltung der Dienstkleidung des Flugpersonals und der Grafiken für die Innenausstattung.

Die Sonne
El Al identifizierte sich ebenfalls mit der für das Land berühmten Mittelmeersonne. Als die Innengrafiken für das Jumboflugzeug Boeing 747 gestaltet wurden, haben wir dem Farbschema das Bild der Sonne – orange, rosa, rot, silber und weiss – zugrunde gelegt und sind damit dem Wunsch des Unternehmens gefolgt, die Passagiere mit den warmen Farben Israels zu begrüssen.

C'est à partir de ce point-là, que la direction de la compagnie El Al s'est rendu compte que l'entreprise possédait une nouvelle personnalité qui, après une phase d'évolutions successives, avait acquis des traits bien définis. En 1979, nous avons reçu mandat de composer un manuel sur le logotype et les fournitures et publications de l'entreprise; le nouveau logotype intégré et la nouvelle gamme de coloris étaient dès lors définitivement établis et devaient être appliqués par tous les services de la compagnie aérienne à partir du 1er janvier 1980. Ainsi était née une identité d'entreprise qui reflète la fierté nationale et l'histoire d'Israël, le soleil et les couleurs de ses paysages, et l'ensemble des activités de l'entreprise.

Avec l'inclusion du Boeing 747 à la flotte El Al, nous avons reçu mandat de créer les uniformes de l'équipage et la conception graphique de l'aménagement intérieur.

Le soleil
El Al s'est également identifié avec le soleil méditerranén si typique pour le pays. Lorsque nous avons développé la conception graphique de l'aménagement intérieur du Jumbo Boeing 747, nous avons choisi la palette des couleurs du soleil – orange, rose, rouge, argent et blanc –, répondant ainsi au vœu de la compagnie qui souhaitait accueillir ses passagers par les couleurs chaudes d'Israël.

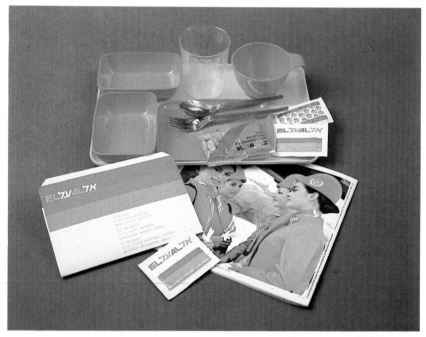

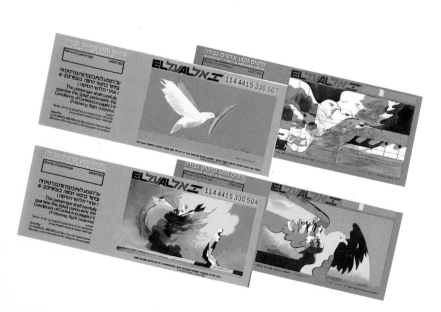

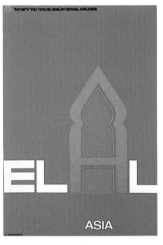

ASIA

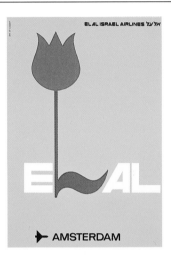

AMSTERDAM

COPENHAGEN

ZURICH

LONDON

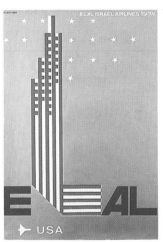

USA

ISTANBUL

CANADA

PARIS

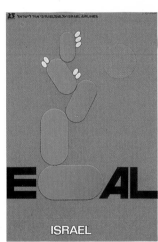

ISRAEL

Our initial involvement with El Al was in the early sixties, when we were commissioned to design a series of twelve destination posters. This was part of a campaign to introduce the two separate Hebrew and Latin character logos designed by Otto Freuman and George Him.

Unsere Tätigkeit für El Al begann in den frühen sechziger Jahren, als wir damit beauftragt wurden, eine Serie von zwölf Hinweisplakaten zu entwerfen. Dies war Teil einer Kampagne, um die zwei verschiedenen Logos mit hebräischen und lateinischen Buchstaben einzuführen, welche von Otto Freuman und George Him gestaltet worden waren.

Nos premiers travaux pour El Al remontent au début des années soixante: nous avions alors été chargés de créer une série de douze panneaux de destination, dans le cadre d'une campagne ayant pour but de lancer les deux logos distincts (l'un en hébreu et l'autre en caractères latins) conçus par Otto Freuman et George Him.

Impressum

Author and graphic design
Wolfang Schmittel

Translations
Silvia Rüggeberg, English
Denise Anne Schai, French

Responsible for publication
Konrad Baumann

General production
Offset+Buchdruck AG, Zurich

Color separations
Cliché+Litho AG, Zurich

© 1984 by ABC Edition, Zurich
ISBN 3-85504-080-X
Printed in Switzerland

Impressum

Autor und grafische Gestaltung
Wolfgang Schmittel

Übersetzungen
Silvia Rüggeberg, englisch
Denise Anne Schai, französisch

Verlegerische Gesamtleitung
Konrad Baumann

Gesamtherstellung
Offset+Buchdruck AG, Zürich

Fotolithos
Cliché+Litho AG, Zurich

© 1984 by ABC Verlag, Zürich
ISBN 3-85504-080-X
Gedruckt in der Schweiz

Impressum

Auteur et conception graphique
Wolfgang Schmittel

Traductions
Silvia Rüggeberg, anglais
Denise Anne Schai, français

Direction de l'ouvrage
Konrad Baumann

Production générale
Offset+Buchdruck AG, Zurich

Photolithographies
Cliché+Litho AG, Zurich

© 1984 by ABC Editions, Zurich
ISBN 3-85504-080-X
Imprimé en Suisse